Barkerville Quesnel & the Cariboo Gold Rush

Barkerville Quesnel & the Cariboo Gold Rush

Gordon R. Elliott

Order this book online at www.trafford.com
or email orders@trafford.com

Most Trafford titles are also available at major online book retailers.

First published in 1958 under title: Quesnel, commercial centre of the Cariboo gold rush.

Print information available on the last page.

ISBN: 978-1-4120-9487-0 (sc)

Trafford rev. 08/07/2019

Trafford
PUBLISHING® www.trafford.com

North America & international
toll-free: 1 888 232 4444 (USA & Canada)
fax: 812 355 4082

Foreword to the 2006 Edition

In the years since the publication of Gordon Elliott's *Quesnel, Commercial Centre of the Cariboo Gold Rush* in 1958,[1] much has happened in the history of Quesnel, and much has stayed the same. The community has weathered the ups and downs of British Columbia's boom/bust economy and, in Elliott's estimation, remains one of the most important towns in the Cariboo. Perhaps more than any actual events that have taken place in the North Cariboo in the intervening years, however, it is our understanding of history itself that has shifted. We no longer, for instance, think of history as something that is always presented to us in book form. The history of a place does not begin at the moment of European contact, nor with writing. Interest in local and regional history is more widespread than ever before. Since the late twentieth century, moreover, the discipline of history has begun to focus more extensively on its own methodology: historians are keenly aware that the perspectives that they bring to their writing are constantly shifting. Elliott, in discussing the writing of *Quesnel, Commercial Centre of the Cariboo Gold Rush*, is very conscious of how any book of history reflects both the life and times of the historian as well as the time in which it was written.

Of his book, Elliott says, "One day I knew what I was going to write. All I was going to do was to make a point." But our perspective constantly changes, as Elliott notes. He observes, "You change your views about history. When I would go out to Norman Lee's ranch, I would go through the biggest boulders, on the Chilcotin Flats. A few years later, when I was going there to get a horse, I rode it all the way back to Williams Lake, and there were those boulders. The horse was trying to rub me off on the boulders—she was wild—but they weren't nearly as big as I thought they were. Things aren't what they are." Elliott's observation, that where we are situated at a given moment in time influences our views of the past, is partly what makes his book important: it is, among other things, an archive of the mid-twentieth century. Some of the language and ideas may seem dated, but they reflect the spirit and sensibility of the era in which they were written. Any history is ultimately a story that we tell ourselves; in Western traditions, it has usually been created, and brought alive for a reading audience, through writing. But the writing had better make for a good story. As

---

[1] The book was later reissued under a different title in 1978 when it was called *Barkerville, Quesnel and the Cariboo Gold Rush.*

Elliott asserts, "If you don't do the writing well, you're not going to bring it [history] into being."

Elliott's enthusiasm for his subject matter in *Quesnel, Commercial Centre of the Cariboo Gold Rush* shows itself in the widely varied sources that he uses to bring alive the history of the North Cariboo, and in the way that his language invites readers into an earlier world of British Columbian experience. A vivid description of the "Hurdy Gurdy Damsels" in a letter sent to the *Cariboo Sentinel* in the mid 1860's, James Anderson's Barkerville poetry, and a detailed account of the devastating Barkerville fire written by photographer Frederick Dally in 1868, for instance, give us a book that is at once a "good read" as well as a valuable historical document. The book should also dispel any stereotypes of Canadian regional history as being somehow "boring." Of the Barkerville fire, Dally notes, for example, that, "The fire was caused by a miner trying to kiss one of the girls that was ironing and knocking against the stove displaced the pipe that went through the canvas ceiling, and through the roof, which at once took fire. This information I got from an eye-witness who never made it generally known, thinking that it might result in a lynching scene." These kinds of details contribute to a sense of the cultural and social history of the region. They move us beyond the sense of "big H" History as the account of "great" events and "great" people. Instead, Elliott gives us a slice of the everyday life of the times while simultaneously highlighting significant events in the formation of the town of Quesnel, and the development of the surrounding area.

Elliott's history was first published in 1958, the year of British Columbia's centennial. The 100th anniversary of the province also marked the declaration of Barkerville as a provincial heritage site; the book's timeliness thus also reflects a developing interest and pride in local and regional history. The history of the book's evolution, moreover, itself mirrors what was happening on the provincial scene at the time. Elliott's interest in regional history developed during his work at the Provincial Archives in Victoria, while he was in graduate studies at the University of British Columbia. The provincial archivist introduced Elliott to a variety of primary materials on Cariboo history that had been largely neglected until Elliott examined them. Since Elliott, when he first began his work at the Archives, had been told that, as part of his job, he "had" to write a book, he chose the topic of Quesnel, Barkerville, and the Cariboo Gold Rush.

Quesnel had always been important to Elliott personally. As a child and teenager growing up in Williams Lake during the 1920s and

1930s, "Quesnel," he says, "was where all the action was. It had a theatre; it had a hockey rink. Imagine—a theatre!" From his comments, it is clear that this Cariboo story had always been on his mind. While Elliott's book on Quesnel had begun as an educational tool for children in grade school, local interest, as well as the provincial government's centennial support, resulted in his re-writing the book for an adult audience. This proved a painstaking process: Elliott went through every passage in the original text, and re-wrote each one, typing out the new passages and gluing them onto the original manuscript.

The beginnings of Quesnel reach back to the mid-nineteenth century and the town's development was intimately connected with the migration of people to the North Cariboo during the gold rush of the 1860's. In fact, Quesnel is one of the earliest settlements in British Columbia—the "city" at the forks of the Quesnel and Fraser Rivers. While the town of Barkerville may have been the geographic centre of the Cariboo Gold Rush, Quesnel was its commercial centre. In many respects, Barkerville created Quesnel, as Elliott's book points out, and the town's development was integral to the economic success of Barkerville. Elliott had initially planned to write a history of all of the communities comprising the Cariboo, beginning with Barkerville and Quesnel, then Williams Lake and Clinton, continuing southward until he finished his writing in Squamish, where his family lived when he was born. Elliott is now in his eighties and is still actively involved in British Columbia's book scene; he is currently working on his history of the Williams Lake area.

Yet, despite a talent for writing, Elliott considers himself more of an editor than an author. He has edited numerous books focusing on British Columbian regional history, including *Pemberton: The History of a Settlement* (1977); *Memories of the Chemainus Valley: A History of People* (1978); and *Exploring the Coast By Boat* (1979). In addition, Elliott edited the 1968 edition of *Klondike Cattle Drive: the Journal of Norman Lee* and prepared the 2005 edition of that book for publication, as well as co-writing *Pick of the Neighbourhood Pubs: A Guided Tour in British Columbia* (1986). Elliott was a longtime friend and editor of the famed Canadian novelist Margaret Laurence, among others; his involvement in writing and publishing in Canada now reaches back more than half a century.

Perhaps it is finally Elliott's own richly layered personal history that best illuminates the diverse nature of British Columbia's Cariboo region. Elliott is not a typical academic or historian, though his scholarly rigour is evident in everything that he does. When his parents were first married, Elliott's father ran a pack train that followed the Canadian Pacific Railway route; his mother was a school teacher in Pemberton. Elliott was born at St. Paul's hospital in Vancouver. Shortly thereafter, he and his family moved to Williams Lake, where he spent his formative years. After serving time in the airforce during World War II, he attended the University of British Columbia from 1948–1954. He also completed two years of doctoral study at Harvard University but then dropped out because, he said, "It was all American and British and German. Not one course on Canadian history" Elliott was always interested in the lesser known and often overlooked details of Canadian regional history; his scholarly focus on these areas was years ahead of its time.

Despite a lengthy teaching career at both the University of British Columbia and at Simon Fraser University, where he was one of the first faculty hired into the English department, Elliott's academic career, he insists, was, "Luck. Straight, pure, and simple luck." Yet, I would argue, it is not luck at all: Elliott has a unique ability to blend the world of the academic with a practical understanding of the place that is British Columbia. While Elliott may not be fluent in Greek or Latin truly, he does, as he says, "know how to get on a horse"—but he also knows how to "do" history.

Blanca Schorcht
Quesnel, 2006

TABLE OF CONTENTS

PREFACE

Barkerville, Quesnel, and the Cariboo Gold Rush was first published in 1958 by the Cariboo Historical Society as *Quesnel, the commercial centre of the Cariboo gold rush.* It was not a chronological history of the region, but a topical one which attempted to explain why the hamlet at the junction of the Quesnel and Fraser rivers developed and why it prospered while others flourished and then decayed. But that flourish and that decay constituted the background against which Quesnel grew, and in order to relate the history of Quesnel one must also relate the history of Barkerville.

The fact that this history deals with Barkerville and the gold rush generally, more than with Quesnel specifically, accounts for the change in title. The book was out of print for many years, but was so often quoted and consulted that Douglas & McIntyre felt that it should be brought back into circulation. I have done no new research, though I have revised the text and have tried to find some new illustrations. Some of these from the earlier edition, however, are still most pertinent.

The first manuscript for this work was written in 1952 as a volume in a "heritage series" proposed by the Provincial Department of Education, and the work was done in Victoria at the Provincial Archives, which holds all the documents, journals, books and newspapers on which the text is based. I wish again to thank the Minister of Education and the Provincial Archivist of 1958 for releasing the original manuscript for publication and now want to pay a belated tribute to a forward-looking provincial government for having conceived the idea of the heritage series as early as 1950. I again thank the staff of the Provincial Archives who have always been so helpful and so friendly, and this time I particularly thank Barbara McLennan who quickly recognized some of the publishing problems and co-operated so readily and so practically.

The success of the first edition was due in great part to the hard work, diligence and initiative of Naomi Randall of Quesnel, who spent more time than she could afford in doing the index and in acting as my liaison with the Cariboo Historical Society. She has been just as diligent, just as hard working, and just as filled with joy this second time around, twenty years later.

Gordon R. Elliott
Vancouver, B.C.
March 1978

The Legacy of the Gold Rush

The past and present of Cariboo began when prehistoric forces made New Caledonia's gold-bearing mountains, made the valleys and the rocks, and made the river which enabled men to go to them, Tacoutche Tesse. Our present and our past began on the tree-covered mountains and treacherous rivers with Mackenzie as he sought a route from the Pacific—"From Canada by land"—and with Fraser who followed the great river to the sea. These men unveiled economic possibilities that prompted the great fur trading companies to move in.

The Northwest Company and the Hudson's Bay Company made the first contacts with the native Indians and built up a social and economic climate of trust. Many company men, including James Douglas and Daniel Williams Harmon, married women with Indian blood and, by example, encouraged further social relationships between natives and newcomers. As a result of this long and slow and gradual introduction to the white men, and through well established and well ordered fur trading practices, the Indians easily accepted the later invasions of gold seekers with little opposition and very few real confrontations. The Waddington massacres are often cited, but only because they were exceptions. When John McLean camped at the mouth of the Quesnel and tried to cook his bread and beans, he found the Indians to be an irritant, but they caused him no trouble. Peter O'Reilly's sensitive laying out of the

Indian reserves in 1881 possibly also helped smooth the way for social interaction.

But the lure of gold is what created a colony on the outer edge of the world, created the province of British Columbia, and helped create, in part, Canada itself. Before the rush for gold, New Caledonia was a geographical expression controlled by the Hudson's Bay Company, but in late 1857 a Company boat carried gold to San Francisco, along with news that gold had been discovered on the Fraser River. That news spread quickly and widely. Miners came in droves from all over the world. Leftover forty-niners from California, drifters from Oregon Territory, disappointed farmers from Vancouver Island. Men from Australia; men from China; men from England, Scotland, Ireland and Wales; from France and Spain and Mexico. Men from the Canadas and the Maritimes. These men were young, adventurous, intelligent, skilled, and foolhardy. And many seem to have had the luck of the gods—at least until they reached the goldfields. This influx of men changed the huge region politically, socially, and economically.

The Fraser River rush began in the spring of 1858, and on November 19, 1858 a proclamation ended the Hudson's Bay Company monopoly and created a new mainland colony, British Columbia. As the miners spread over the new colony, the old colony of Vancouver Island, though prospering as a jumping-off spot and administrative centre, saw itself losing control of the potential wealth of the mainland because newcomers were promoting easier trade from New Westminster. Both poorly populated colonies recognized the cost of double administration at a time when Cariboo's gold rush was finishing and they were facing a depression; in 1866 the two colonies were united as British Columbia.

As the depression settled in, the many gold seekers began looking for solutions to their economic problems, and the push from the goldfield areas, especially from Barkerville, was for becoming part of the 1867 Canadian confederation. Men from the Canadas and the Maritimes, men such as the Overlanders who had been raised on Responsible Government, were not at all satisfied with an appointed Legislative Council, and wanted a more mature form of government. These Canadians also had emotional links with eastern Canada and some, such as Francis Jones Barnard, were already thinking of physical links: if not of a railroad, at least of a wagon road to Lake Superior. The influence of all these men was felt at the Yale Convention in 1868 which favoured British Columbia's becoming a Canadian province, which it did in 1871.

Besides new forms of government, the gold rush wrought a new society. No longer was the only civilized sound in New Caledonia the sound of bagpipes at Fort Alexandria. Towns appeared, and as each of these "fairs" grew, flourished and decayed, another took its place, each "better" than the last. The earliest town, Quesnel Forks, was rough and tough, and the government must have thought that the population of the place would remain totally male, for the government built a jail with no accommodation for women. Barkerville was much less rowdy, with its dance halls, stores, haberdasheries, churches, restaurants, bakeries, hotels, banks, assay offices, schools. A library, a theatre, a newspaper, a hospital. All the amenities. Barbers, doctors, dance hall girls, preachers, lawyers, shysters and sharpies, law-abiding family men with their respectable wives lived there, and the social democracy which prevailed seems to have been passed down over the years. Wellington D. Moses was a black barber, but had a place in this goldfield world; so did the Chinese, or Celestials who, though having few legal rights, were so numerous that no one could ignore them and they became, right from the beginning, part of the social fabric of the province.

As the towns created by the gold rush were taking on an appearance of permanence, there was improvement in transportation for bringing in even more men and supplies. Captain Irving's steam ship has gone, as has Oppenheimer's mule train and Dirty Harry's bull team, but stage coaches still travel the roads, as do great freight trucks, and the road they follow to Cariboo is very close to the road of 1865. It still goes from Yale to Alexandra Bridge, along the river to Boston Bar and on to Lytton, to Spence's Bridge, to Clinton, and up and over the 83 Mile Hill to the 100 Mile House and past Felker's and the 141, along G.B. Wright's road to the 150 Mile House. It by-passes Frank Way's and Soda Creek now, but still goes over the Alexandria prairie, down the hill and across the river into Quesnel, through Cottonwood and on to Barkerville. Our great north road of the past is our great north road of the present, a legacy from the gold rush. As are such names as Huston and Tingley and Hamilton.

This great influx of argonauts also created a need for some kind of law and order, and the colonial system of justice which grew also had its social implications. Under Judge Begbie, and under Chartres

Brew and his policemen, the colony lived by a rule of law, by a respect for the law enforced and administered by a network of justices of the peace who became powerful figures in the communities. As a result the colony and the province established a name for a rough and ready justice, but one which was fair to all: black and white, Oriental and Occidental, American, Canadian, or European.

Out-of-work miners had always been supported by a continuing fur trade, but that fur trade has almost gone, though some furs are still taken. Evidence of our fur trade past remains in a few old log buildings, traces of the brigade trail, brigade pastures; in place names like Alexandria, Williams Lake and Lac La Hache; and in family names like Ogden and Twan. Lumbering was also of importance in the old days, but for local use—for erecting growing towns, wagons, sleighs, flumes, and bridges. Wood products in one form or another, rather than gold, are now the main source of Cariboo incomes, and the mills which export lumber for use a half a world away.

Local agriculture continues to be important, and land clearing along the river indicates that agriculture is expanding. Flour milling, however, has gone; Adams's Soda Creek mill and Collins's Hawk Creek mill are discernible only by those who knew them before, the stones having gone into the river or to a museum. But many of the early farms still flourish: the Australian and Kersley and the Hudson's Bay lands at Alexandria. Most of the old road houses are gone and the new road construction has by-passed others as well as reduced the distances between them, but some farms established as stopping places on the wagon road are still recognizable: Lansdown Farm, for example, and Cottonwood House, which is now owned by the Provincial government and operated as a museum. And the country still has its Johnstons and Yorstons and McInneses and Moffats and Bakers.

An understanding of the Cariboo gold rush is essential to any real understanding of British Columbia. The gold rush lasted a long time, really, with ups and downs, from 1858 to 1945, and some of the characteristics of Ben MacDonald, who turned the first gold at the mouth of the "Canal," were the same as those of Fred M. Wells, who set off a new rush in the 1930s. The gold rush might indeed have had psychological effects on British Columbia, which is still bursting with economic and social change as more and more newcomers arrive in the "golden" west.

CHAPTER ONE

Geography and First Inhabitants

The valleys, rocks, and blue hills of Cariboo were creations of pre-historical times. Once a sea covered the entire northwest of North America and deposited layer upon layer of sediment; below, a subterranean heat melted older materials which then surged upward as igneous rock. Seventy million years ago the sea receded, dry land emerged, and the earth's crust folded eastward to make our mountain ranges. The distant Rockies, like the Cariboo range, were so created, and in some places molten rock pushed through the surface to become basaltic columns, and mountains of granite rose not far from outcroppings of gold-seamed quartz. With a new surface appearing and rains falling, rivulets and streams and rivers sped their ways through the low areas, cutting valleys, carrying away the soft silt, and leaving the hard rock to be further weathered by wind-carried sands, expanding ice, snow, and more rain.

Temperatures changed, snows became heavier. As the snow increased it packed into ice, in some places two miles thick. Ten thousand years ago, when temperatures increased once more, these glaciers disappeared. The river then formed battered its way through ravine and rock, cut valley and canyon, and made a way to the sea. This river became known as the Great River or Tacoutche Tesse or, as we now know it, the Fraser—the main drainage river of Central British Columbia and the Cariboo.

The Fraser rises in a small lake, Cowdung Lake, at the western base of the Rocky Mountains, flows northward and westerly in the Rocky Mountain Trench, and carries waters from tributaries that flow westward from the Rockies, or eastward from the Cariboo Range. One main tributary from the east out of a mountain-bound valley is the McGregor River. Beyond the junction of the two, but as though in an extension of the McGregor Valley, the Fraser turns south where only a few miles separate the Fraser from Summit Lake drained by the Crooked River into McLeod Lake. That water reaches the Arctic Ocean after becoming part of the Parsnip, Peace and Mackenzie rivers. The great, muddy Fraser then meets the Willow from the south, the Nechako from Stuart and Francois lakes, and continues south through canyons of rock, then through soft clay soil, picking up mud and debris. About seventy miles below the Nechako the West Road River flows from the western mountains, the barriers which force water east to the Fraser or west to the Dean River and Pacific Ocean. South again from the West Road, later called the Blackwater, the debris-laden Fraser beats a way through the canyon at the mouth of the Cottonwood and meets the Quesnel River which has been flowing northwest from Quesnel, Beaver, and Horsefly lakes. Immediately before emptying into the Fraser, the Quesnel flows a short distance west, then south, and again due west to pour its clear water—water that has been passing through rocky country rather than through clay—into the great river. The junction so formed is almost a "U." The Fraser continues south through clay banks or cuts a way through barriers of rock. Sometimes the river carries a great deal of water, sometimes a little; at certain seasons sand bars appear. The muddy river which is joined by the grey Chilcotin, the clear Dog Creek, the sparkling Thompson, bursts through the Cascade canyons, flows quietly at last, and lays silt in a great, rich valley to form a perfect delta as it reaches the Pacific Ocean just north of the 49th parallel.

The Cariboo district covers a region of rolling upland—hilly in places—cut by deeply eroded troughs, with tiers of bench-land at varying intervals and heights between the stream beds and the plateaux. The Fraser flows around the Cariboo in the north and through it in the centre, while eroding a deep channel 1,000 to 2,000 feet below the upland and the benches of rich soil. Eastward the plateau rises gradually from 3,500 to 5,500 feet in the Cariboo Mountains, the main watershed of the area. This area may be divided into two levels: that below 2,000 feet and that at 3,500 feet or over. The former comprises the large valleys and plateaux of preglacial times; the latter elevated part centres in the Barkerville area where there are many rounded mountains and flat-topped ridges, with Mount Agnes reaching 6,200 feet and Mount Tinsdale 7,027 feet. This division is the source of streams issuing from confined valleys into more level ones or onto stream plains such as those at the Quesnel, Cottonwood and Willow.

The climate of the district is continental. Summers are dry and warm with a mean temperature of 56°F (16°C). Nights are cool. Rainfall increases progressively towards the mountains, and summer frosts occur at higher altitudes. Winter lasts from mid-November until mid-April with an average snowfall of two or three feet and mean temperatures of 21 degrees F (—5°C) at Quesnel. Snowfall is greater, rainfall higher, and temperatures lower in the mountains to the east. Barkerville, with an altitude of 4,180 feet, has a frost free period of 52 days, while Quesnel, at 1,549 feet, has one of 102 days. Such climate, combined with rough, glaciated soil, does not make for great forests. Those of Cariboo are of lodgepole pine, spruce, small fir, birch and cottonwood, though farther east from Quesnel, in a higher rainfall area, cedar appears and spruce becomes larger. Cottonwood and poplar grow chiefly in the valleys.

Quesnel is located at the junction of the Quesnel and Fraser rivers, in the "U" formed by them, almost on the 53rd degree of latitude. The commercial centre of the Upper Cariboo, the town serves the settlements of Cinema, Strathnaver and Hixon to the north; Nazko to the west; Kersley, Australian, Alexandria, Mac-alister and Marguerite to the south; Wells and the old Cariboo settlements of Cottonwood, Stanley and Barkerville in the mountains to the east. On the west side of the river are the growing settlements of Buck Ridge, Castle Rock and Narcosli Creek. In earlier times Soda Creek was part of the economic unit, but today Soda Creek is more closely related to Williams Lake. Beaver Lake, Horsefly, Likely and Keithley Creek, too, are influenced by that community to the south.

The Cariboo—a corruption of "car-boeuf," or elk—is a region that has never really been defined, but certainly early settlers did not think of it as so vast a region as people think of it today, though each and every person seems to have a different idea of where the Cariboo begins and ends. Some people consider Lillooet and Cache Creek and Clinton to be in the Cariboo; others say the Cariboo begins at the top of the 183 Mile Hill. Some include the Chilcotin, others include Prince George. When the miners came to the area in 1859 and 1860, however, the term indicated only a region north of Quesnel Forks and Keithley Creek, of which Barkerville became the centre. The mouth of the Quesnel River was not even then considered to be in the Cariboo. Before the miners, when the first missionaries arrived and when the Hudson's Bay Company was operating Fort Alexandria, the area was merely an unspecified part of New Caledonia and administered from Fort St. James. New Caledonia itself embraced all land from the Rocky Mountains westward to the sea. The area had been so named by North West Company men sent to locate trading posts in this great new area which had been discovered by Alexander Mackenzie in 1793.

We do not know when man first went into Cariboo although Coast Indian tribes may have gone there thousands of years ago. At any rate, natives were there long before white men arrived. These natives, of a different ancestry than the Coast tribes, called themselves Dénés, meaning "Man," and the Dénés themselves divide into four main tribes: the Sekanais living in the Rocky Mountains, the Babines of the Babine Lake area, the Chilcotins of the Chilcotin country, and the Carriers living in the Nechako Basin and along the Fraser River.

The first inhabitants of Quesnel were the Carrier Indians, and the first priest in the area, Father Demers, gave an account of them in a letter to his Bishop:

> The men are quite remarkable for their great height and their splendid carriage. The women are large and have a certain corpulence and strength that one does not see in the tribes of the Columbia. They are, also, dressed more decently than the Columbians although the country is no richer in products to make clothes. They have robes of leather or they are quite modestly covered with a skin.

Father Demers also remarked on the name, "Carriers":

> Many suppositions are made on the origin of the name Porteurs [Carriers]. The most accredited is that these savages not having any beasts of burden, carry their baggage on their backs when going from

one place to another. Undoubtedly, this French name has been given them by the voyageurs in the service of the Company. And yet the women are the servants of their husbands who choose to load them with the heaviest burdens.

Another idea of the name Porteurs is inspired by certain customs practiced among this nation and among another here. After the death of their parents [later writers say their husbands], they burn the bodies and gather the bones into leather sacks which for three years they carry with them. And so the name of Porteurs. The spot where the body has been burned is carefully covered with bark in the form of a lodge and surrounded by an enclosure or a row of stakes. The bones are drawn from the leather sack at the end of three years in order to be deposited in a great, coarsely manufactured box which is fastened as solidly as possible to the end of the posts, "ad perpetuam rei memoriam." This imposing ceremony completed, a funeral feast is given to which the parents and friends of the deceased are invited and the burial is completed.

Their primitive religion provided for a future life and a vague Supreme Being with his spirits. The "Shaman" or "medicine man" was supposed to drive away the evil spirits by incantation, and through this supposed supernatural power he became master of the people.

Father Demers was obviously appalled by conditions:

The usual nourishment of these people is the salmon that ascends the Fraser River and its tributaries in immense quantities. They dry it in the sun in order to save it for winter and even for several years. It is admirable foresight for these savages who have no theory or practice of any culture and who inhabit a sterile country whose climate is severe. With the exception of a few localities exploited by the Company the soil is uncultivable: the winters are long and severe; frost lasts even into the month of June and sometimes entirely destroys the country's harvest.

The life of these savages does not exceed sixty years, I have not preventing longevity among these people, one can place first, their kind of nourishment and the dirt in which they wretchedly live; and in the second place, their habits which brutalize them and engender almost always fatal illnesses for lack of care and the removal of the causes which produced them. The third cause that destroys their constitution, is their manner of sheltering themselves from the weather. They make themselves miserable hovels in the ground which have only an opening for the smoke to escape and through which they can enter or leave only by means of a long piece of notched wood which serves them for ladder or stairs. They are crammed in these dens about a fire whose smoke is suffocating and whose heat does not protect them from the raw damp ground about them and upon which they stretch themselves.

Life had gone on in such a manner for centuries before the white man arrived. The earliest report of the area though is 1745 when the Chilcotins destroyed the village of Chinlac at the junction of the Nechako and Stuart rivers and massacred the Carriers. By this time white man was settling California. Within a short time the sea fringe of New Caledonia was attracting attention. Not much later the land of the Carrier too was invaded by curious Europeans. After settlement had been established, and after British Columbia had passed from colonial to provincial status, Peter O'Reilly, Indian Commissioner and former magistrate, reserved various lands of Cariboo for the Indians. At Quesnel in June 1881, for a total of sixty-two Indians O'Reilly reserved sixty acres on which a village stood on the east bank of the Fraser River about two miles below the town of Quesnel, itself situated on the site of an earlier Indian settlement. He allotted as well an adjoining 1,320 acres at Quesnel, and another 235 acres known as "Rich Bar." The outlet of Dragon Lake he also reserved. O'Reilly's report tells why he did so:

> ...this [the outlet of Dragon Lake] they especially prize as the source from whence they obtain their supply of white fish through the winter months.
> The several burial grounds as pointed out by the chief have been defined and reserved; they are considerably scattered, some being within the town site of Quesnelle.
> These Indians were especially pleased with the arrangements made for them in regard to their land, and expressed their thankfulness through their Chief "Baptiste."

The burial grounds within the town site included, according to O'Reilly's report, "A grave in Quesnelle Town, between Front Street and the Fraser River....A grave on lot 4, block 8, Quesnelle Town....A grave in the middle of a field belonging to Mr. Danielson [Fernbrook Farm] on the left bank of Quesnelle River....A graveyard on the left bank of Fraser River, about a mile above the town, partly in a Chinaman's field...."

CHAPTER TWO

Exploration and First Settlement

During the eighteenth century, Spain, Britain and Russia were all interested in the west coast of North America and had done considerable exploration along the coast of what is now British Columbia long before any white man had set foot into the interior. The rivalry between the three countries was intense, and the British after 1776 recognized the possibilities of American expansion to the west. This idea was also growing in the great fur trading companies which became willing to finance westward exploration in order to lay claim to the fur bearing regions. The North West Company absorbed the XY Company and became the great exploring force in the west, and one of its lesser partners came to the fore to be considered one of the boldest explorers on this continent. Alexander Mackenzie, a Scot from Stornoway, discovered the river which bears his name, but was disappointed to find it draining north to the Arctic rather than west to the Pacific. Three years later he made a second attempt to reach the Pacific by land, and did so on July 22, 1793.

The winter of 1791-92 Mackenzie spent in England perfecting the mathematical knowledge he deemed necessary and arranging the purchase of technical equipment for the long and hazardous trip. On October 10, 1792 he left Fort Chipewyan on Lake Athabaska to winter on the Peace River six miles above the mouth of the Smoky.

That winter he spent in collecting furs to be sent to Fort Chipewyan, his main base, and in observing the local Indians, but chiefly in attending to the many details required for his journey into the unknown. By May 8, 1793 he was ready; on the following day ten men without a guide, but with two Indians to act as hunters and interpreters, stepped into a single canoe and their voyage began.

Up the Peace and over the rapids to the forks of the Finlay and Parsnip, and remembering the advice of an old Indian, Mackenzie took the south fork. The work became increasingly difficult, so difficult that the hardy men were exhausted by six in the afternoon and felt compelled to stop then instead of at sunset, but they were moving again by five in the morning. Unfortunately the explorers missed the Crooked River leading to McLeod and Summit lakes, and as a consequence missed a short portage across the divide to the great river "flowing toward the midday sun," but which did not, natives told them, flow into the sea. Instead, the adventurers followed the Parsnip to its headwaters and, on further redirection, went "817 paces" to a small lake, on to the Bad River, now known as the James, and to the McGregor River. On June 17th they shot into the main current of the "Great River." "Tacoutche Tesse," Mackenzie called it; the Columbia he thought it to be.

Mackenzie passed the most direct route to the Pacific when in the early morning haze of June 19th he did not see the Nechako River, but continued downstream past the West Road, Cottonwood and Quesnel rivers. At this last one he had his initial experience with the Carrier Indians who had never seen a white man before, but had had unfavourable reports of him from the coast.

Carrying bows, arrows and spears, they lined the bank of the river and threatened the party with death if it landed. The explorers swung to the other side of the river to camp, but Mackenzie won the confidence of the Indians before pushing downstream. At the point now known as Alexandria the voyagers found seven families of Indians dressed in leather and beaver or rabbit skins. Here they stayed two days.

Once more relying on Indian advice and against his own inclination, he then turned northward for a more direct and easy route to the sea. Mackenzie realized that both time and supplies were running out and that he must return before winter to Fort Chipewyan. For this reason, he had to take the shortest route.

On June 23rd the party faced north, and on July 3rd, after having been delayed by a search for bark and gum to repair the canoe, they turned up the West Road River. After one day Mackenzie decided to abandon the canoe and to proceed overland on foot. This he did, and nearly three weeks later inscribed his now famous lines on a rock above the salt water of Bentinck Arm: "Alex Mackenzie From Canada by land 22d July 1793." They began the return journey the following day. By August 4th they were on Tacoutche Tesse once more; by August 17th on the Parsnip; by August 19th on the main stream of the Peace; and five days later at their winter quarters to report the crossing of the continent by land.

Although Mackenzie was the first white man to see the Great River and its adjoining country, another man explored it to its mouth. Simon Fraser, like Mackenzie and others of the early explorers of this province, was a "Nor'Wester," but unlike so many of the others who were Scottish, he was of United Empire Loyalist stock. Fraser took possession of the territory west of the Rockies under the name of New Caledonia and, at Fort McLeod in 1805, established the first permanent trading post. A year later, following Mackenzie's route up the Parsnip and down the Bad River, as Mackenzie had named it, he caught his first sight of Tacoutche Tesse, the river which was to bear his own name within a few years. He did not miss the Nechako, and with a certain scorn suggests that Mackenzie was lax in his duty in having done so. Fraser went up the Nechako to found Fort St. James on Stuart Lake and later, on Fraser Lake, Fort Fraser. Towards the end of the following year, 1807, he founded Fort George at the confluence of the Nechako and Great rivers.

In the fall of that year Hugh Faries and Jules Maurice Quesnel arrived with supplies from Montreal and orders from Fort Chipewyan. Americans were exploring to the southwest and the North West Company had to explore as great an area as possible and establish itself as far south as possible in order to preserve its fur trade. Fraser was to follow the great river to the sea—although the mouth of the Columbia was known, the land the Columbia drained was unexplored and uncharted. Too late to begin that year, he occupied the long winter months in preparing at Fort St. James. On May 22, 1808 the company of twenty-four left Stuart Lake in four canoes and went down what the leader referred to as the Fraser River, but which is now called the Nechako, the name the Indians had given it centuries earlier. The explorer had already traversed this route several times and therefore made no notation of this part of the trip in his journal, but on May 28th, after a one-day stop at Fort George, the company launched its canoes into the strong, sweeping current of the "Columbia," and thence began one of the greatest adventures on this continent—Fraser's voyage to the sea.

Fraser's day-to-day journal describes the hazards and hardships, and readers feel for themselves the courage required to journey down that hitherto-unconquered river. At Fort George the voyage began on the broad sweep of the innocent-looking river, but even on the first day, in the Fort George Canyon, "against a precipice which forms the right bank of the river," one of the canoes was damaged and almost lost. Fraser learned through experience, and on arriving at Cottonwood canyon lightened the canoes before running the rapids; with a backward look when through he named them "La Décharge de la Montagne."

Downstream the company swept, and at sunset came to a clear river which Fraser later indicates that they named the Quesnel River. Here they encamped.

At 5 a.m. Monday, May 30, 1808 the party embarked once more and passed through charming country well inhabited by Indians, a country "interspersed with meadows, hills, dales and high rocks [which had] on the whole a romantic and pleasant appearance." They came to the Stella-yeh of the Carrier tribe and to a point just above Soda Creek in the Atnah territory. Although these Indians were friendly themselves, they warned of hostile tribes farther south, down-river, but Fraser was determined, and on June 1st, after a day of surveying the first rapids, the voyagers sped down them, wrecked a canoe, and spent the rest of the day portaging to avoid further destruction.

The trip south from this point was one of terror, horror, grief and joy, and ends with Fraser's great disappointment at not seeing the main ocean, and with his discovery that he had not travelled to the mouth of the Columbia but to that of a different river. Past the Chilcotin they went, almost to Pavilion Creek and on to that "dreadful chain of...insurmountable difficulties" which the party surmounted only by leaving canoes and travelling along Indian paths. Past the Lillooet Indian encampment, on to Lytton, mostly on foot but occasionally in boats hired from natives, feasting on berries, salmon and roots, and sometimes on dog meat, the party worked its way.

From Lytton to Cisco rapids by water; then they scrambled over what Fraser called with unparalleled understatement "a very steep hill." Rather than portage the dugouts that were so much heavier than the customary birch bark, some of the voyageurs decided to risk the river rather than carry them. One such experience sufficed. In the Black Canyon, Fraser reported that "one of the Indians climbed to the summit and by means of a long pole drew us up, one after the other." At Hell's Gate, he said, "[we could] scarcely make our way with even only our guns":

> It is so wild that I cannot find words to describe our situation at times. We had to pass where no human being should venture; yet in those places there is a regular footpath impressed, or rather indented upon the very rocks by frequent travelling. Besides this, steps which are formed like a ladder or the shrouds of a ship, by poles hanging to one another and crossed at certain distances with twigs, the whole suspended from the top to the foot of immense precipices and fastened at both extremities to stones and trees, furnish a safe and convenient passage to the Natives; but we, who had not had the advantages of their education and experience, were often in imminent danger when obliged to follow their example.

Through Spuzzum they went, through the Little Canyon to Yale where he learned that the river was navigable to the sea, and on through the great valley to Musqueam village close to the mouth. A day later, on July 3rd, farther yet down-river, Fraser took observations and settled once and for all that the river was not the Columbia. He was disappointed. And yet he seems to have been more disappointed in not having seen the main ocean after having "gone so near it as to be almost within view...."

The return journey they commenced on the same day, July 3, 1808. As well as with hostile Indians along the banks of the hostile river, Fraser had to contend with indications of desertion and near mutiny among his own men. On July 8th he reached Yale, on the 14th Lytton, on the 20th Pavilion Creek, and on the 25th the Chilcotin. On August 1st, Tuesday, they set out early and "debarked at Quesnel's river, where we found some of the Natives, from whom we procured some furs, plenty of fish and berries—continued our route until sunset."

At this point on May 29th, on the downward journey, Fraser had sent Quesnel to reconnoitre. The journal says that the "country around" had

> a very fine aspect, consisting of extensive plains, and, behind these, hills rising over hills. The trees in this quarter are pine, cypress, birch, hemlock, cedar, juniper, etc. At night flashes of lightning accompanied with loud peals of thunder, and heavy rain.

Simon Fraser's lieutenants on this undertaking were his valued friend John Stuart, and Jules Maurice Quesnel. The latter was born in Montreal in 1786, the second son in Joseph Quesnel's family of thirteen. The father was a poet and dramatist who had been born in St. Malo, France, and who had come to Canada in 1779 and taken out naturalization papers a few years later. Jules Maurice joined the North West Company as a clerk and in 1804 was stationed at Edmonton. In 1811, after his trip with Fraser, he left the service of the Company and returned to Upper Canada where he carried on a trading partnership with St. George and Baldwin, the latter a relative of Robert Baldwin who gained fame in the uprisings of 1837. After amassing a fortune Quesnel retired to Montreal with his wife, the daughter of an independent trader from the northwest, the former Marie Josephte Cotté whom he had married in 1816. In 1838 he was appointed a member of the Special Council of Lower Canada, and three years later a member of the Legislative Council under the Union. He died on May 20, 1842.

The North West Company was not slow in exploiting New Caledonia and in a short time forts Fraser, McLeod, St. James and George were shipping furs east. The Company, however, soon had a rival. In 1811 the Pacific Fur Company under the leadership of John Jacob Astor of New York founded the post of Astoria at the mouth of the Columbia River. This company too realized the value of the interior as a fur trading area and sent David Stuart north from Astoria to establish forts. After founding several posts, the chief of which was Fort Okanagan, in 1811 Stuart discovered the Indian village of Kamloops where he remained until the spring; then, after consultation with the partners of the company, he established a fort there. The North West Company, jealous of its power, sent men into the same area and in 1812 it too established a fort at the "meeting of the waters." In November 1813, when the North West Company purchased the Astor group, Kamloops came under the sole ownership of the Canadian traders. The fur trade was then turned westward by way of the Okanagan Valley to the Columbia, through Astoria to England, or to China, in the *Isaac Todd*, the company's new ship.

When the trade was apparently going to have its outlet in the south and west rather than the east through Fort Chipewyan, another post between Fort George and far-away Fort Kamloops was essential. One of the most important posts in New Caledonia was constructed on the great brigade trail at the head of navigation and called Fort Alexandria after Alexander Mackenzie. This North West Company fort about twenty-one miles above Soda Creek and on the east side of the Fraser was located at the most southerly point reached by Mackenzie before turning north on his search for the Pacific. This fort became the transfer point for supplies going north by brigade to Fort St. James and other forts in New Caledonia's fur bearing region. Return trips brought the treasure in fur. At this point goods were transferred from pack animals to boats which shuttled up the river to the other forts. In 1821 the Hudson's Bay Company and the North West Company amalgamated under the name Hudson's Bay Company, and all forts in Canada then came under jurisdiction of the new company. The original Fort Alexandria was abandoned at this time and superseded that year by a new fort, Alexander, some miles farther north, but in 1836 the fort was again moved, to the west side of the river to serve the trade of the Chilcotins better. In 1863 Colonial Secretary W. A. G. Young felt that he was obeying custom and respecting tradition when he officially renamed the fort "Alexandria."

John McLean was sent there at the end of March 1837, but was moved to Fort St. James at the end of May by Peter Skene Ogden, Chief Factor. The Stuart Lake post with its dreadful solitude almost drove McLean to despair. In contrast, the post at Alexandria was, he wrote,

> agreeably situated on the banks of Frazer's [sic] River on the outskirts of the great prairies. The surrounding country is beautifully diversified by hill and dale, grove and plain; the soil is rich, yielding

abundant successive crops of grain and vegetable, unmanured; but the crops are sometimes destroyed by frost. This charming locality, the friendly disposition of the Indians, and better fare, rendered this post one of the most agreeable situations in the Indian country. In spring, moreover, the country swarms with game—pheasants and a small species of curlieu in the immediate vicinity, and ducks and geese within a short distance. The sport was excellent, and, with the amusement the cultivation of my garden afforded me, enabled me to vegetate in great comfort. . . .

The Fort operated until 1867 and Hudson's Bay Company maps show its location as late as 1872 but by that time it had, in reality, closed. In his 1863 survey of the projected Waddington route from Bentinck Arm, Lt. H. Spencer Palmer saw the fort as a "half ruined cluster of log dwellings roofed with mud, [which] stands on the right bank of the Fraser, on a bench about fifty feet above the river and 1470 feet above the level of the sea. . . ."

The Company eventually executed a quit claim of its rights and John S. Twan obtained a Crown Grant of 109.5 acres covering the original site of the Fort. His father had been an employee of the Company; in fact his ancestors, as he himself used to say, had been in the service of the Company for 200 years. Twan (who died in 1947), fearing the walls would collapse and injure someone, had in 1922 razed the buildings and used the logs for firewood.

CHAPTER THREE

The Gold Rush

For years the Hudson's Bay Company held a monopoly on both Vancouver Island and in New Caledonia. Fur was the mainstay and the old company discouraged permanent settlement of the area fearing, rightly, that the fur trade would be ruined with the coming of colonists. But news of gold discoveries could not be silenced. To thousands of men in California and Oregon, men who had seen the end of gold there, men who were drifting northward, hoping, this was welcome news.

The discovery of gold in New Caledonia is surrounded by uncertainty. To say by whom or at what place gold was first found is impossible, but some people say that McLean, the Hudson's Bay factor at Kamloops, bought gold from Indians as early as 1852. Generally conceded, however, is that John Houston, a Scottish sailor who caught the "goldbug" in California, discovered gold on Tranquille Creek in the spring of 1857. His findings were sold to the company at Kamloops, sent to Victoria, and from there to the mint in San Francisco. Because the gold passed through so many hands, the news could not be denied and in July 1857 Gov. James Douglas wrote officially of the discovery.

William "Billy" Ballou saw the possibilities and rushed southward to prepare for an express company. The news spread, but too late in the year for anything of importance to take place. The great Fraser River Gold Rush began the following spring, and between twenty and thirty thousand miners and campfollowers took $543,000 in fine gold dust from the river during the year 1858, although disappointments were great and many. Those finding no fortune on the river, but with still enough money to pay their way south, left the region, dubbing the rush "The Fraser River Humbug."

But not all left. With the idea that the source of this fine gold would be found in coarse deposits farther up-river, a thin line of men began working its way north, over the difficulties encountered by Fraser a half-century earlier: Hope, Yale, Boston Bar, Thompson, Lillooet, Pavilion, Fountain—all great names, but mere indicators pointing towards the "mother lode." In 1858 Aaron Post was already at the mouth of the Chilcotin, but turned back. In the spring of 1859 Peter Curran Dunlevy and a party arrived at the same place.

Dunlevy was more fortunate that Post. Here on a sand bar a Hudson's Bay Company runner, an Indian on his was to Fort Alexandria, told Dunlevy of gold on a little river northeast of Lac La Hache. The prospectors scanned a map that the Indian, Tomaah, sketched on the sands and they arranged to meet him sixteen days later on the brigade trail at the southeast end of Lac La Hache. The party immediately turned downstream towards Lillooet, and went through Marble Canyon and over to Kamloops to buy supplies.

Peter Dunlevy, Tom Manifee, Tom Moffitt, Jem Sellers and Ira Crow were Americans unfamiliar with the policy of the Hudson's Bay Company and were surprised when the factor refused to sell to them because they were prospecting in the fur region. The fur domain had to be preserved: the company could well afford to lose white trade to save Indian trade. Through the engaging personality of Dunlevy, however, the policy was broken and the group arrived back at Lac La Hache with the required supplies. At the rendezvous within the allotted time, the argonauts met Tomaah and another Indian, Long Baptiste, the man who eventually led them to the first of the great Cariboo prospects. Tomaah was attracted to a young Taghleil girl at the encampment and had left the party.

This group panned the first gold on the Horsefly River in the middle of June 1859. Twelve hours later another group arrived: Hans Helgesen, George Black, Joe Devlin, Duncan McMartin and Neil Campbell. The rush by the Horsefly route had started.

The Lac La Hache trail was not popular, and therefore the trek up the river continued. In May of 1859 James Twan was a small boy of six years standing on the jetty at Fort Alexandria watching a Prince Edward Islander, Benjamin MacDonald, shove off into the river and steer north to the first great, clear stream coming into the Fraser on his right. The daughter of the local factor had told Mac-Donald where he would find the yellow sand. On June 3, 1859 MacDonald turned the first shovel of pay dirt on the Quesnel River. That summer about a thousand men worked the muddy Fraser between Alexandria and Fort George; the wise ones had turned east up the Quesnel.

On July 15 *The British Colonist* of Victoria reported the discovery of gold "on a small creek, called Canal [Quesnel] River. . . ." The story was not believed. Two weeks later a letter appeared in the same paper:

> We are located on the Canal River, about twenty-five miles above Fort Alexander, I want you to see John M. Inge, George M. Paine, Tim Matterson, Frank Wright, and Ben Jones, and tell them to come up here. I think there is hiyou gold up here, and if you and the boys come you had. . .better buy enough grub to last you until cold weather sets in. . . .
>
> Johnson. . .says he is lying flat on his back with his heels cocked up towards the heavens, taking it easy, waiting for the water to fall . . . .Ben MacDowell [Ben MacDonald?] thinks that he can make ONE HUNDRED DOLLARS per day when the water falls. He has made as much as fifty dollars per day.

The newspapers were skeptical since the "humbug" of the Fraser, but the following spring the hordes went to the Quesnel River to see for themselves, went to the forks of that river, spilled over the mountains, found gold and shipped it to Victoria. The newspapers at the coast were jubilant. They carried articles on gold to the point of boredom, for they had sent "on the spot" reporters to give their readers full and exaggerated coverage. The rush lasted five years.

From the forks of the river, sixty miles from the mouth, a short route was found to Fort Alexandria, and the old fort thrived as the supply base for the fields of Cariboo, as the new region was called. The draw of gold depopulated the areas between Hope and Lytton, and by 1860, belatedly it is true, the Fraser River gold fever had reached China. The "Celestials," as the Chinese were called, entered the colony by the shipload to pan dust considered by the whites to be too fine, and they scattered along the Fraser and up the Quesnel as far as the forks. At Fort Alexandria, in 1860, there were stores, a post office, storage buildings and saloons. Its heyday was short-lived as a distributing centre, and even the following year people questioned Gold Commissioner Philip Henry Nind's wisdom when he staked a townsite and prepared to sell lots. Only half a dozen men remained there; the post office had been withdrawn earlier because the mails were being sent to Williams Lake. There was no gold at Fort Alexandria which was off the beaten track—a new and better route had been found to the new and thriving town at the forks of the Quesnel River.

Quesnel Forks, Quesnel City, the Forks, or just Quesnelle, as it was variously called, was the earliest locality to develop into a permanent camp. The "city" was built on a flat at the foot of the mountains separating the two branches of the Quesnel River, the houses facing the waters of the south fork. A narrow levee barely wide enough for the unloading of pack trains ran along the front of the settlement. By 1860, twenty or more houses, ten or twelve stores, boarding houses, whiskey shops and tents were cramped on a ten-acre clearing. The next year Dennis Lynch constructed the government building, a single-roomed log house with two cells. This jail must have been intended for a purely masculine company for not until a month after it had been built did the first of four white women arrive.

That same year lots were to be surveyed and the townsite laid out properly, but Col. R. C. Moody, Chief Commissioner of Lands and Works for the colony opposed the work and had it deferred. He saw that parties in mining districts group themselves hurriedly together in what may be called towns, but that they were not permanent. Already that year Alexandria, the little town across the river from the fort, had dropped to a population of two men: T. La Rocque, a French-Canadian, and Charles Train, a Frenchman.

It is common rumour [Moody wrote to the Colonial Secretary] that the so called Town of Quesnelle will shift its population in the spring to another site more suitable in the estimation of the miners, packers and store keepers.... A mining town is in truth for a long while more the character of a prolonged "Fair" than anything else.

Moody did not oppose the building of a bridge by W. P. Barry and S. Adler, nor the running of a ferry by Capt. J. Mitchell, for he knew that great strikes were being made in the mountains and that means had to be effected for crossing the river. Mitchell was the first to advocate a road from the Forks to the mouth of the river, but it was not built. Barry and Adler constructed a 200-foot bridge across the Quesnel at Forks City and charged a toll on people and goods coming from Williams Lake through Beaver Lake to the gold fields.

By 1861 Beaver Lake was an established stopping place. As early as April two stores had been erected, one by J. Deshields and another by Dunlevy and Sellers. These last two intrepid miners had decided that they could make more out of mining with a stopping place, a gambling house, and a supply station than they could with a shovel. Moffitt and Manifee were assistants. The great laden pack trains passing through made Beaver Lake well known as an animal market: on September 1, 1861, François Guy sold a team of fifty-eight mules and four horses. Single animals sometimes sold for as much as $300.

The miners pushed over the hills and up the north fork. By the time the town was developing at the Forks, W. R. "Doc" Keithley and J. P. Diller made their strike high on a bluff above the high-water mark of Keithley Creek. They conveyed dirt from their stakings to the water by a chute and washed by rocker. George Harvey had been with them, but went to Harvey Creek alone, built sluices and prospered. "Doc" stayed, but sold after mining the first claim successfully for a short time.

A reporter from the *Colonist* said that by October 1860 the gambling halls were full blast on both Keithley and Harvey creeks. By July the next year, F. Black and W. Carlyle had a store at the mouth of Keithley, and R. Davis had one seven miles upstream. The community that grew at the mouth of this creek became known as Black's Store, but with true prospector's optimism, a move was afoot to rename it "Cariboo City." Nevertheless Moody was right: Keithley, too, was soon a thing of the past. John Rose, George Weaver, "Doc" Keithley and Ben MacDonald, the original dis-coverer of gold on the Quesnel, struck paydirt on Swamp Creek, and those 3,000 men who had swarmed over the banks of the Quesnel in 1860 left it to the Chinese. Soon the centre of the gold world became the town on Antler Creek. Quesnelle Forks, Keithley, and Swamp River were dead.

Antler consisted of eight or ten houses in 1861, one of them the first board building in Cariboo. Each new place coming to life drew people from the dying town before it, and Antler, as the centre of a busy crowd, became the new metropolis. Houses were erected every day, and the bar-keeps, traders, packers, restaurant owners and gamblers from Quesnelle City located there. The forks was deserted and remained so until the end of September when miners moved for the winter; the prosperous ones made the journey to Victoria or San Francisco, the less fortunate wintered at the Forks, Beaver Lake, Williams Lake, or Alexandria. Money lost its value in this new city of one long, narrow street lined with whiskey shops and loafers, where travelling minstrels, roulette, monte or draw poker amused weary men. On a level spot above the town was R. P. Baylor's sawmill. When the town was surveyed, the Gold Commissioner found the mill to be improperly located and ordered it removed to the sawmill flat. As each building was moved the land was turned over in a frantic search for gold.

By 1862 the end of Antler was in sight. Antler and Keithley followed a somewhat similar pattern: a year or two of hectic life, a short but rapid period of decay, then buildings torn down in order that men could mine the ground on which the buildings had stood. By August that year Antler was at that point where decay is making itself felt, but is not yet obvious.

Like Quesnel Forks, Antler was superseded. H. Tilton, Richard Willoughby and the Patterson brothers discovered Great Lowhee Creek and in the first two days panned out $5,200. Then William "Dutch Bill" Dietz made his great strike on Williams Creek—so named after him—and this became the focal point for gold miners of the world—the great city of Cariboo. But before becoming so well known, it too had rivals.

In 1861, in the spring, William Cunningham struck pay dirt on Cunningham Creek. He had been one of the discoverers of Lightning Creek, and the Cunningham Claim on Williams Creek, although one of the first above the canyon, was paying as late as 1865 when the peak of the excitement was paling. When Cunningham died at Soda Creek on June 21, 1864 from mountain fever he had taken more gold from Cariboo than had the fabled Cariboo Cameron, whose name had been more conspicuous in Cariboo annals. The tragic circumstances surrounding Mrs. Cameron's death, the subsequent sleighing out of the frozen body and the bags of gold to Victoria, the shipment to and burial in Ontario and the later unhappy events are more widely known because of greater publicity at the time. But Cunningham was one of the men who announced to Antler that gold had been discovered on Van Winkle Creek. The exodus from Antler began.

The town growing at the junction of Van Winkle and Lightning creeks was promised a fair future. A new route to the mines was rumoured and already trails were being cut from the mouth of the Quesnel River through Beaver Pass. The government predicted Van Winkle would be the depot for the whole of the mining district. Because a Rip Van Winkle Bar near Lytton in earlier days had been prosperous, the new locality was given this name as a token of both honour and prediction; by mid-August 1862 the predictions were becoming fact. There were log houses, bakers, shoemakers, blacksmiths, hotels, saloons and gambling houses. The Bishop of Columbia, no less, was preaching every Sunday to a congregation that included three ladies with their families. The government looked into the future, and Judge Matthew Baillie Begbie received tenders for the construction of a court house and jail. Early promise was not realized. The government proved to be wrong. Within three years the crowds had gone. One hotel remained, that of N. L. McCaffrey, and one grocery store, that of Johns and Cahn, supplied the area with foodstuffs, dry goods and liquor. McCaffrey was also the postmaster, but in 1868, because he had not been paid regularly, he discontinued this service and the office was not re-opened until July 1, 1872.

All these places were eventually eclipsed by the trio of towns on Williams Creek: Richfield, above the canyon; Barkerville, immediately below the canyon and sometimes called Richfield Lower Town; and Camerontown. Of Richfield only the court house remains. Billy Barker's town lives on. Nothing remains of Camerontown.

"Dutch Bill's" strike started the three, and before long, a

town about the same size as Antler, but superior to it, was built on Williams Creek. The houses were better than those of Antler, more roomy and built "as if folks calculated on remaining." By the spring of 1862 three or four saloons were open and twenty more were nearly finished and ready for their stocks. In describing Richfield— for the town had received a name from Lt. H. Spencer Palmer, the surveyor—one writer of the time said:

> ...nothing [is] wanting that could possibly be procured to appease the appetite of the hard working miner; but if his pocket cannot come up to relieve the cravings of his appetite, he must be content to live on what is styled Cariboo turkey (bacon), and Cariboo strawberries (beans), and a happy man is he whose pocket can command this nutritious though simple fare. As for myself I have left my partiality for delicacies in Victoria, to be unpacked and called in requisition when I again reach the vicinity of the St. Nicholas or the French Hotel.

The average price of the "nutritious though simple fare" was $2.50 a meal. Money meant little, and letters such as one dated Williams Creek, Cariboo, May 18, 1862, increased the stampede to the northern fields of gold:

> Dear Joe,
>   I am well, and so are all the rest of the boys. I avail myself of the present opportunity to write you half-a-dozen lines to let you know that I am well, and doing well—MAKING FROM TWO TO THREE THOUSAND DOLLARS A DAY! Times good—grub high—whiskey bad —money plenty.
>   Yours truly,
>   Wm. Cunningham.

Richfield grew first and burst at the seams; Camerontown was named before Barkerville in the presence of Judge Begbie; and for some time people thought Barker's town might prosper better with the name "Springfield." The same conditions prevailed in the three towns, for in reality together the three were one long town with a break at the canyon, one long street with sidewalks of different grades, and in some parts, where a sidewalk was most needed, none existed. The hills on each side of the creek were covered with tents and shanties of a mining population estimated at upward to 10,000. The shanties or cabins of log and mud usually had tin stovepipes, but no windows. They were, as one writer said, neither "Doric, Ionian, nor Corinthian, but decidedly Columbian." The first glass to be used, other than in saloons, was that imported for the court house at Richfield—$3 for a pane 8 inches by 10 inches.

CHAPTER FOUR

Barkerville

Although Richfield grew first and Camerontown was named before Barkerville, Richfield and Camerontown were too cramped and the last of the trio became the metropolis of Cariboo. William Barker, more successful than those miners working above the canyon, sank a tunnel into a narrow ledge and forty-eight hours later emerged with $1,000 in gold. Around this hole the town grew. A contemporary writing of Richfield in August 1863 described its houses as verbs, "neither active or passive, but certainly regular, irregular and in some cases defective." The houses were the same at Richfield Lower Town, as Barkerville was sometimes called. However, "some wish to call it Springfield, others Barkerville; if we admire the trails which lead to it, and the different springs which help to keep the same, in some places, a complete puddle...I should say it was an appropriate name...." The following year, merchants came and erected wooden buildings, generally of whipsawed lumber, in an irregular fashion on an irregular street. Because the creek was subject to freshets and flash floods most of the houses were on log posts, and hardly two of the houses were the same height. Consequently, the sidewalks in front were at varied elevations and made walking unsafe. Overhead business signs protruded over the muddy, filth-strewn, hole-pitted, 18-foot wide street.

The town had everything necessary for community life; if not the best, then a good substitute. There were laundries, blacksmiths, butchers, bakers, piemen-turned-masseurs, barbers, churches, saloons and hotels; a theatre, a newspaper, and a cemetery. Wellington D. Moses, the Negro barber who wrote his own intriguing advertisements for his own brand of guaranteed hair restorer, wrapped a bleached pine pole with red flannel in lieu of the traditional painted barber pole.

The *Cariboo Sentinel* which carried Moses's advertisements began publication on June 6, 1865. Published on a hand press that weighed only 275 pounds and which had been brought to New Caledonia in the 1840s by the Roman Catholic Church, the newspaper was a flamboyant, newsy and entertaining paper appearing every Saturday at first, and later twice each week. Its purpose was to reform the town and the government, and to publish miners' grievances. Selling for $1 a copy, the four pages gave value for money with European, Canadian, American, Cariboo and local news. Mining information, celebrations, death notices, advertisements and jokes were scattered throughout the pages. In the first issue an advertisement for Fell and Company's good coffee appears between an item telling that Surveyor General J. W. Trutch had arrived from England and another item announcing the birth of a son to the wife of Sergeant McMurphy at Lochlomond House. Directly below this is a death notice: "On Williams Creek, on the 13th ult., John G. Fraser, C. E., late of Canada."

Today one of the most interesting sections of what remains of Barkerville is the old cemetery which indicates the variety of countries, creeds, nationalities and even temperaments represented in the gold area. Chinese were not buried with the rest of the community. Except for the "Celestials," the mining population tolerated any colour or race, all being buried together. The remains of the late John G. Fraser were probably interred above the Cameron Claim, in the little Camerontown cemetery to which a road was built by public subscription. In 1866 there were nine unknown, unmarked graves; until that time no complete record was kept of burials.

The cemetery site was selected by John A. "Cariboo" Cameron and his foreman, James Cummings, early in 1863. Cameron's claim was immediately below the site and Cameron himself now rests in this plot, overlooking his old claim. Chartres Brew, Gold Commissioner and County Court Judge, is also there. Judge Begbie, supposedly, composed the epitaph on Brew's headboard; after the words had been cast in lead they were nailed onto the plain wooden board. It stands today. The first grave in the plot, or at least the first registered grave, was that of Peter Bigson of Vankleek Hill, Canada West, who died of mountain fever, or typhoid, on July 24, 1863, aged 31. The grave was dug by Cummings.

Life was rough in the camps: typhus was prevalent, there were no lights near the mines, and cave-ins were common. Only the young and healthy could survive. Sometimes they too died. The ages given indicate a young man's country. Dr. W. B. Wilkinson, the first surgeon at Quesnel and the man who attended Mrs. John A. Cameron in her last illness, was thirty-five; S. P. Parker from England, thirty-seven; David Whiteford from Scotland, thirty-three; George Johnston, Nova Scotia, thirty-six; William Giles, Missouri, thirty-six; James Binkett, Wales, thirty-one; Emily Bowron, wife of John Bowron, was from Michigan, age thirty-five; Thomas R. Patullo, father of T. D. Patullo, a premier of this province, was aged forty-two. Joseph Park, an exceedingly clever lawyer, was only forty-nine when, too drunk to travel from Richfield to Barkerville in January, he fell in a flume on Williams Creek and died the next day. John McLaren, B.A., from Kingston University, was killed by a cave-in in the Ballarat drain, age thirty-one.

All types and all trades were represented on the roaring creek. J. B. Malanion was a violinist who had played with the Paris opera, but here was a carpenter by trade who taught music to some of the Barkerville boys. John McLean, a hotel keeper in Quesnel at a later date, told the story of Malanion's death:

> When he was dying in the old Cariboo Hospital in a bed next to his lay O. G. Travaillot, also dying. Both knew they could not survive the night, so true to the last to the spirit of the camp, they wagered fifty cents as to who would die first. Toward morning Malanion's voice rang out clear as a bell: "Captain Travaillot, you win. I lose. I die now." His head dropped even as his voice rang out.

Williams Creek was fortunate in its medical assistance, and a hospital was soon built. Dr. Wilkinson was in the area, having returned to medicine from mining when the need for a doctor arose on the creek. John Evans, leader of a group of Welshmen who had come to seek their fortunes, wrote that "much sickness prevails amongst us, about half the number are complaining from Rheumatism.'' The miners held a meeting when conditions became unbearable, and in 1863 the hospital was opened by subscription. Consisting of one ward, doctor's office and kitchen, it fulfilled necessary duties with collections and government grants.

For amusement in town the people raised another subscription for a library and requested that the government supply a site at Camerontown. The government complied and in 1864 John Bowron became its first librarian. Three years later, when Camerontown had declined, the library was moved to Barkerville where the reading room had a ''well selected and diversified stock of books.'' Private libraries also existed on the creek; the Occidental Cigar Store had novels, while the Roman Catholic and Anglican churches had books of a more serious nature.

Theatricals too were popular and the Theatre Royal became a focal point of town. Perhaps the saloons were the brightest spots and the most interesting to students of social history a hundred years later. They served meals and liquor, had dance halls and card rooms. Here the more serious amusements were forgotten and dancing with the Hurdy became the popular sport.

Because of the shortage of women, an enterprising businessman brought a party of German girls from San Francisco to sell their dances in the mirrored saloons. The girls were escorted to the mines in 1866 by Madam Bendixon and employed by several saloons. After each dance the girl and miner went to the bar where he paid a dollar for ''something'' for himself, and fruit juice for his partner who collected 50¢ a drink from the bartender the next morning. When Barry and Adler opened their new saloon in 1867 they advertised eight girls. Nothing indicates that the Hurdies were anything more than dancers.

At first the music was supplied by a hand organ or ''hurdygurdy,'' but a piano was later packed from the mouth of the Quesnel River. The *Cariboo Sentinel* printed a letter written from Williams Creek to the coast papers:

Hurdy Gurdy Damsels

There are three descriptions of the above named ''Ladies'' here, they are unsophisticated maidens of Dutch extraction, from ''poor but honest parents'' and morally speaking, they really are not what they are generally put down for. They are generally brought to

America by some speculating, conscienceless scoundrel of a being commonly called a "Boss Hurdy." This man binds them in his service until he has received about a thousand per cent for his outlay. The girls receive a few lessons in the terpischorean art, are put into a kind of uniform, generally consisting of a red waist, cotton print skirt and a half mourning headdress resembling somewhat in shape the top knot of a male turkey, this uniform give them quite a gortesque [sic] appearance. Few of them speak English, but they soon pick up a few popular vulgarisms; if you bid one of them good morning your answer will likely be "itsh sphlaid out" or "you bet your life."

The Hurdy style of dancing differs from all other schools. If you ever saw a ring of bells in motion, you have seen the exact positions these young ladies are put through during the dance, the more muscular the partner, the nearer the approximation of the ladies' pedal extremities to the ceiling, and the gent who can hoist his "gal" the highest is considered the best dancer; the poor girls as a general thing earn their money very hardly.

Hurdy Fiddlers

This class of musician (pardon the misnomer) have also a school of their own, in which melody and euphony have no part. Noise is the grand object. The one who can make the most noise on the fiddle, and shout his calls the loudest, is (amongst the hurdy artists) considered the most talented. Sometimes to increase the power of an orchestra (which seldom consists of more than two violins—more properly Fiddlers in this case), they sing and play, and in passing up Broadway, Barkerville, in the evening, you may hear them letting off steam as if their lungs were made of cast iron, and the notes forged with a sledge hammer.

James Anderson's "Letter to Sawney" in the *Sentinel* of July 23, 1866 was in a similar vein.

Last simmer we had lassies here
Frae Germany — the hurdies, O!
And troth I wot, as I'm a Scot
They were the bonnie hurdies, O!

There was Kate and Mary, blithe and airy,
And dumpy little Lizzy, O!
An' ane they ca'd the kangaroo,
A strappin', rattlin' hizzy, O!

They danced at nicht in dresses light,
Frae late until the early, O!
But oh! their hearts were hard as flint,
Which vexed the laddies sairly, O!

The Dollar was their only love,
And that they lo'ed fu' dearly, O!
They didna' care a flea for men,
Let them coort hooe'er sincerely, O!

They left the creek wi' lots o' gold,
Danced frae oor lads sae clever, O!
My blessin's on their "sour krout" heads,
Gif they stay awa for ever, O!

CHORUS—Bonnie are the hurdies, O!
The German hurdy-gurdies, O!
The daftest hour that e'er I spent
Was dancin' wi' the hurdies, O!

Much of Barkerville is gone, some by the fire of 1868, the rest by decay. The "Letters to Sawney," however, can restore a great deal to us for they reflect an economic and social picture of the town from 1863 until 1871.

James Anderson was born in Perthshire, Scotland, in 1838 or 1839, of a prominent family and, as indicated by his writing, received a good education. He married in 1860, a son was born the following year, and James Anderson was lured to Cariboo in 1863. Anderson made no golden fortune, but his personality made him many friends. He could sing or write and often read his own works in the public lounge, or at concerts and entertainments. He and a friend published a weekly manuscript they read aloud at gatherings, and from time to time the *Cariboo Sentinel* published his verse. In 1868 the Barkerville press printed a selection of his poems, and a second edition appeared in 1869. A Toronto firm brought out his material in 1895.

The "Letters to Sawney" in Scotland from his friend "Jeams" in Cariboo were not Anderson's only contribution to Barkerville's social life. As the *Sentinel* said, "He was one of the original members of the Amateur Dramatic Association, and by his vocal talents rendered much assistance at their performances, his songs being always much admired." He wrote new words to old country tunes, to tunes that everyone knew and these songs he wrote into his plays. Sometimes the music too was written by people right there on Williams Creek. Not all of his poems are in the Scots dialect, but those giving the best picture of life during the Great Cariboo Gold Rush are.

"Jeams" was not one of the fortunate who took a fortune home. In November 1871 James Anderson left Barkerville and returned to Scotland. He settled on one of his father's properties, moved eventually to England, and died there in 1923. His last poem before leaving the creeks included the following lines:

> 'Twas all I asked of thee,
> One handful of thy plenteous golden grain,
> Had'st thou but yielded, I'd have sung "Farewell!"
> And home again.
>
> But, time on time, defeat!
> Ah, cold and cruel, callous Cariboo!
> Have eight years' honest persevering toil
> No more of you?

Old Barkerville had everything necessary for community life: dances and card games; churches and pool halls; hotels and saloons; a theatre, a hospital. All the amenities were there, even "gamblers and courtesans, and strange to say, one of the latter keeps a licensed house. — O tempora, O mores!" Probably the maddest town in North America in its time, it did not last many years.

On September 16, 1868 Barkerville went up in flame. The fire began in Barry and Adler's saloon near the centre of town at 2:30 p.m. on a cold, dry day, and in just one hour and twenty minutes from the first cry of alarm, according to the Sentinel, the last roof fell and the destruction was pronounced complete. The story was carried by the local paper, the premises of which were destroyed with the rest of the town, but which began publication in another location soon afterward. We learn from the newly located paper that the fire was rapid and looting was common, but no fatal accident or personal injury occurred. Little attempt was made to curb the fire because no organized group was in charge. In reference to the origin of the conflagration that cost almost $700,000 in goods alone, the Sentinel said:

there can be no doubt as to its accidental character; nor can there be the slightest blame attached to any person, as the light and inflammable character of the roofing of the entire town was such that in an extraordinary dry time like the present, it is only a wonder that such accidents did not occur almost daily....

Another eye-witness to the destruction of the town was Frederick Dally, a photographer who had opened shop in the rowdy town. He had left Victoria on June 21st and, having arrived on the creek July 21st, was established only a short time before his premises were destroyed. On the day of the great blaze he had been visiting a former steward on the *Cyclone*, the ship on which Dally had travelled from England. He later wrote an account of the fire:

By the number of stove-pipes very close together, coming through the wooden roofs of the building at every height and in every direction, that were sending forth myriads of sparks and numbers of them were constantly alighting on the roofs where they would remain many seconds before going out, and from the dryness of the season, I came to the conclusion that unless we shortly had rain or snow to cover the roofs, for they remain covered with snow all winter, that the town was doomed....

The morning of the fire was bright and clear and the sluice boxes...bore traces of a hard frost as the icicles that were depending from the flumes were two or three yards in length....Although trade was somewhat dull, still it was steady and profitable....little did I think that in less than two hours, not a vestige of the town would remain but a burning mass of ruins. I gave him [Patterson off the *Cyclone*] an invitation to visit my new building, just finished and nicely furnished.

I...seated myself in a chair and again meditated on the probability of a fire when I heard several running on the plank sidewalk and heard one exclaim, "Good God! What is up!" I ran instantly to see the cause of the alarm and to my astonishment beheld a column of smoke rising from the roof of the saloon adjoining the steward's house. I saw the fire had a firm hold of the building and, as there was no water to be had, I felt certain that the town would be destroyed. So I collected as much of my...goods as possible together, and hastened with them to the middle of the creek, and left them there whilst I made several journeys after other goods. The fire originated in a small room adjoining Barry & Adler's saloon. One of the dancing girls was ironing and by some means or other, the heat of the stove-pipe set the canvas ceiling on fire, which instantly communicated with the roof and in less than two minutes the whole saloon was in flames which quickly set the opposite building, the Bank of British North America, in flames.

So the fire travelled at the same time up and down both sides of the street...and although my building was nearly fifty yards away from where the fire originated, in less than twenty minutes it, together with the whole of the lower part of town, was a sheet of fire, hissing, crackling, and roaring furiously. There was, in a store not far from my place, fifty kegs of blasting powder and had that not been removed at the commencement of the fire, and put down a dry shaft, most likely not a soul would have been left alive of the number that was then present. Blankets and bedding were seen to be sent at least 200 feet high when a number of coal oil tins, 5 gallons, exploded, and the top of one of the tins was sent five miles and dropped at the saw-mill on Grouse Creek.

Every person was thinking of his own property and using desperate efforts to save it, and some not placing it sufficiently far out of reach of the element had all consumed, and others again had it taken so far out that during the time they were away trying to save more property, Chinamen and others were stealing from them as fast as they could carry it away. One stout Chinaman showing too many creases about him that did not look quite natural, the police made him strip, and off came six shirts, two pairs of draws, three pairs of trousers, etc. Another, two coats, three shirts, and two pairs of trousers, etc. Another, two coats, three shirts, and two pairs of trousers. Another had hidden away behind the false canvas wall of his house, over one thousand dollars worth of flour, rice, boots, etc., and every useful article usually sold by storekeepers in the mines.

The town was divided by the "Barker" flume, crossing it at a height of about fifty feet, and as it was carrying all the water that was near, it kept the fire at bay for a short time from the upper part of the town. But the hot wind soon drove those that were standing on it away. The fire then quickly caught the other half of the buildings, also the forest on the mountain ridge at the back. And as the sun set behind the mountain, the grandeur of the scene will not be quickly forgotten by those who noticed it.

And then the cold, frosty wind came sweeping down the canon [canyon], blowing without sympathy on the houseless and distressed sufferers, causing the iron-hearted men to mechanically raise the small collars of their coats (if they had been so fortunate as to save one) as protection against it. Household furniture of every description was piled up along the side of the creek, and the people were preparing to make themselves as comfortable for the night, under the canopy of heaven, as circumstances would allow. And in the early morning, as I passed down the creek, I saw strong men rise from their hard beds on the cold stones, having slept wrapped up in a pair of blankets, cramped with cold and in great pain, until a little exercise brought renewed life into their systems.

At a quarter to three p.m. the fire commenced; at half past four p.m. the whole town was in flames, and at 10 o'clock the next morning signs of rebuilding had commenced, and lumber was fast arriving from the saw mill and was selling at one hundred and twenty-five dollars per thousand feet. The number of houses destroyed was one hundred and sixteen. After the fire I found I had the key of my house in my pocket which reminded me of a circumstance that occurred two years before at a town a mile from Barkerville when a certain Barrister who was in the habit of drinking more than was good for him, when informed that his house was on fire, left the saloon he was in and went and stood on the opposite side of the street to this house and exclaimed, "Never mind boys; never mind! I don't care, let it burn, I've got the key in my pocket." (And so had I.)

The fire was caused by a miner trying to kiss one of the girls that was ironing and knocking against the stove displaced the pipe that went through the canvas ceiling, and through the roof, which at once took fire. This information I got from an eye-witness who never made it generally known, thinking that it might result in a lynching scene.

Dismayed but not defeated, people of Barkerville began the next morning to clear the debris and rebuild. A new town arose, both in character and in appearance. Many merchants who had intended leaving with quick profits were burned out and had little money to erect new buildings. Only those planning permanent business remained. A Williams Creek fire brigade of volunteers came together to wield leather buckets in case of fire. Banks rebuilt; churches grew once more; the library became well established again. All the standard necessities of a town grew anew, but this time in an orderly pattern. The fire occurred on the 16th of September. The *Sentinel* of the 22nd carried a great description of the fire, of the aftermath, and predictions for the future:

> Already are there over thirty houses standing in symmetrical order on the old site, and the foundation of several others laid; and many more would yet have been in the course of erection were it possible to obtain carpenters and tools.... The town when rebuilt will present a much more uniform and pleasant appearance. By the regulations of the local authorities, in concurrence with the people, the

main street has been increased in width fifteen feet and the sidewalks fixed at a regular and uniform grade. Vacancies which were originally intended for cross streets but occupied by sufferance, are now to be left open, and altogether the new town will be much more convenient for business, and will be a decided improvement on the old; and we would not much wonder if in the course of a few years time many who are now heavy losers will cease to regret the conflagration of 1868.

After the town rebuilt, economic conditions closed the smaller operators and over the years the population became less and less. The old town boomed, of course, but in a different manner. In time unused houses were allowed to fall apart, and others were torn down. Occasionally a new one would be built, but only occasionally. Little remains of "new" Barkerville today. The Anglican Church, Kelly's Hotel, and the court house at Richfield are there. The Masonic Hall, the Chinese Temple, the Theatre Royal have gone. So have most of the people.

CHAPTER FIVE

The Overlanders

The Overlanders who arrived in Quesnel in 1862 were part of the only group to cross Canada by land in search of Cariboo gold. True, others had crossed the continent earlier, but this was the first organized party to come by a Canadian route. In 1861 Cariboo yielded about $2,700,000 and such an amount attracted world-wide attention. In April 1862 groups of interested young men started from various places in Ontario, or Canada West, and Quebec, eventually joined together and crossed the Canadian plains twenty-five years before modern transportation. Of all types and professions, they had the two qualities in common necessary for the undertaking—enthusiasm and youth.

All the groups in the party, which totalled 160 people, went to St. Paul, and from there north to Fort Garry by steamer. Some "deserted" at Fort Garry, but seven more joined. For a week they stayed at the fort in order to obtain horses, cattle and Red River carts for the trip to Edmonton. Provisions too had to be purchased: for $3 a hundred they obtained coarse, dark flour, and for 6¢ a pound they bought pemmican, a mixture of buffalo meat and boiled buffalo grease. From Fort Garry the band made its way to Long Lake where the real formation of the journey overland was accomplished. Leadership was essential; Capt. T. R. McMicking was elected captain and a committee of thirteen chosen.

From the Long Lake rendezvous, 97 groaning, creaking Red

River carts, 110 animals and 136 people began the 2,000-mile journey westward to civilization. In the party was a woman with her three children; she and her husband had joined the group at Fort Garry. The cavalcade left Long Lake on June 5th and "dragged its slow length" over the plains, arriving in Edmonton on July 25th where some more of the party dropped out.

While moving, the company had made a file a half-mile long. It had started at 5 a.m., stopped at 12, and went onward again from 2 until 6, depending upon campsites. Later, when closer to Edmonton where days were longer, the party was moving by daylight, stopping for breakfast at 6 a.m. after having travelled for three hours. At night, for protection against Indians, they had drawn the carts into a triangle formation and herded cattle and horses to the inside. The tents made a guard around the outside.

On July 29, the reduced party of 125 set out once more with 150 pack animals, each loaded with 150 to 250 pounds. All bulky and unnecessary articles had been abandoned. A few cattle were driven along for food and fifty pounds of flour were carried for each person. Through swamps and brush the party floundered to the Catholic Mission of St. Ann, some fifty miles from Edmonton. On August 20th they filed through a rocky gateway into the Rocky Mountains, and almost a month after leaving Edmonton, on August 22nd, camped on Cowdung Lake, the source of the Fraser River. They had expected to complete the trip from Fort Garry in two months; three months had already elapsed and they still faced unknown dangers in an unknown land. An entry in McMicking's diary for the following day says, "Killed an ox this morning before starting; provisions become slack; pemmican about done and flour scarce." The following day they ate roast skunk and broke the usual rule of not travelling on the Sabbath. On the 27th they reached Tête Jaune Cache, starving. Shuswap Indians supplied them with salmon and huckleberry cakes.

To this point the Overlanders had had an Indian guide, but neither he nor other Indians could give information about the route ahead. Should they raft the Fraser River, or should they trudge overland to Fort Kamloops? Twenty people, including Mrs. Catherine Schubert and her children, chose the unknown route to Kamloops and reached there on the 13th of October after indescribable hardship. On the 14th, after she had "accomplished a task to which but few women are equal; and, with the additional care of three small children, one but few men would have the courage to undertake,'' Mrs. Schubert was delivered of Rose, the first white girl born in the interior of British Columbia. Mrs. Catherine Schubert died in 1918, ten years after her husband, Augustus. She had on the trip, McMicking wrote,

> exemplified the nature and power of that maternal affection which prompts a mother to neglect her own comfort for the well-being of her child, by which she rises superior to every difficulty, and which only glows with a brighter intensity as dangers deepen around her offspring.

The Fraser River group occupied five days in building rafts, lashing logs together with materials found at hand. These rafts were large enough to carry stock and were called by the names of towns the men knew. The day before the Thompson River group departed, a dugout canoe, along with smaller craft, pushed into the Fraser, followed by the rafts *Scarborough, Huntingdon, Queenston, Ottawa* and *Niagara*. Indians watching sadly from the shore are reported to have sighed and said, ''Poor white man no more!''

A. L. Fortune, one of the men, wrote later: ''The river flowed swiftly and our craft with its cargo of stock and passengers glided with the current.'' But the great rafts were not always to glide smoothly. The huge dugout arrived at the Grand Rapids two days in advance of the leading raft, and the men on board, after losing their provisions and possessions, were exposed for two days to cold, fog, and rain without food, bedding or dry clothing. Three men in two canoes—lashed together and called the *Goderich*—fared even worse. One was drowned; the other two were rescued by A. L. Fortune and W. Sellar. When the *Queenston* neared the dangerous canyon it was decided to leave only enough people on board to man the oars; the rest would portage. When all was ready, the ropes were loosed and the raft, with its men, spun into the roaring current. Thomas McMicking watched from the shore:

> Onward they sped like an arrow. They seemed to be rushing into the very jaws of death. Before them on the right rose a rocky reef against which the furious flood was lashing itself into foam, threatening instant and unavoidable destruction, and on the other side a seething and eddying whirlpool was ready to engulf in its

greedy vortex any mortal who might venture within its reach. With fearful velocity they were hurried along directly towards the fatal rock. Their ruin seemed inevitable. It was a moment of painful suspense. Not a word was spoken except the necessary orders of the pilot, which were distinctly heard on shore above the din and tumult of the scene. Now was the critical moment. Every one bent manfully to his oar. The raft shot closely past the rock, tearing away the stern rowlock, and glided safely down into the eddy below. The agony was over. The gauntlet had been run, and all survived. The issue of the ordeal was announced by an involuntary cheer from the brave hearts aboard the raft, which was heartily responded to by those on shore.

That scene was re-enacted by the rafts following. Four days later they reached Fort George where the men bought food from the Indians and waited to see Williams Charles, the chief trader of the Hudson's Bay Company post. Charles did not come soon enough; after two days the parties made independent arrangements with Indian guides to take them through the Fort George and Cottonwood canyons. The *Queenston* left early on September 10th and by 10 o'clock had reached the Fort George Canyon which was much the same as Fraser had seen it fifty-four years earlier. Thomas McMicking described it:

> The channel is obstructed...for a distance of half a mile, and the broken and rugged banks, with their overhanging cliffs, bear a striking resemblance to those of the great canon [canyon] above Fort George. The most dangerous part of it consists of a shelving rock in the centre of the principal channel, upon which a large body of water was propelled to some distance, and, falling off at both sides, formed a double whirlpool below. All passed through them in safety.

McMicking says they all passed through in safety, but A. L. Fortune, with the *Huntingdon*, the largest of the rafts, feared that his craft would be too long to be handled successfully:

> Ten men volunteered to stay with the raft and hold on the stock with us. Some of us made silent supplication to God for his guiding and protection. Away our raft floated easily giving good opportunity to swing her well from the dangerous island rocks on the right side. Our speed increased, and on we glided between eddies, and then with a leap over the fall, our raft slipped under the water, as the front plunged over.... In a moment the raft was past the fall and all

floating safely down with racehorse speed....Arthur Anderson lost hold of his rope and someone caught him floating off the raft. Our canoe that was lashed to the side of the raft made a clean somersault ....On we went as if running a toboggan down a long and steep incline....As soon as we could the raft was moored to wait for the people who took the land.

Except for James Wattie who had been to California, the *Huntingdon* group for the first time saw Chinese people at work: "They were a wonder to us with their chopsticks, Pigtail and sallow skin." Through China Rapids and the narrow Cottonwood Canyon, threading their way through shallow channels, gravel-bars and sand-banks, the rafts made their way to Quesnel the same day, only three hours apart. R. B. McMicking, on the *Queenston*, the first of the two, records the last day's run:

Thursday, Sept. 11th. We started at 5.10 a.m., quite foggy on the river for some time. Ran on a large rock which gave the Raft a good Rack, a good many scared but no one hurt. Ran the [Cotton-wood] Rapids at 11 a.m. which is a narrow chasm through precipitous rocks, not dangerous for a raft but the swells heavy with one little pitch which rolled the water heavy on the raft but hurt nothing, where a canoe must undoubtedly swamp. Got to the mouth of Quesnel at 2.25 p.m. where there is abundance of provisions, there being two stores & eating Houses & other little buildings, Indian huts, etc....Flour 50 dollars, salt 1 dollar a pound, rice 55 cents, Bacon .75 to $1.00, Beans 1.75, tea 2.00 a pound. The day was very fine and pleasant. I got my supper off a table, the first time in four months at Whitehall store for 1.50.

At Quesnel the Overlanders met disillusioned miners returning from the creeks, and individually the men made their own decisions about whether to go to the mines they had come so far to see, or whether to continue to the coast. Some went in to the mines—like the Wattie brothers who worked with Cariboo Cameron before returning to the east after two years—but some camped at Quesnel and took off down the river again as soon as possible. Some of those returned later, like Robert Burns McMicking who became a telegrapher at Deep Creek, Quesnel and Yale, and like A. L. Fortune who tramped up the road with a fifty-pound pack and, after spending all his money, going into debt, and working for wages to pay off his creditors, again walked to Quesnel in 1865, with no gold, but "much experience." John Bowron came back from Victoria; his first wife, Emily, taught school in Barkerville after they had been married on Williams Creek.

Few were successful as argonauts, but their failure as gold miners might have turned their talents in other directions, and to the ultimate benefit of the province. Coming from a mature political tradition, they brought with them, and introduced, a sense of democratic leadership, and their interest in government led to political change. Many with education involved themselves in local works and administration. John Bowron became Gold Commissioner and Government Agent; Archibald McNaughton became an assessor and collector for Cariboo and postmaster at Quesnel. George Tunstall was Government Agent at Kamloops, and Gold Commissioner at Granite Creek; his sons worked with explosives, and the name is perpetuated in Tunstall Bay on Bowen Island. After being involved in exploration, John Fannin became curator of the Provincial Museum; Thomas McMicking took the job of sheriff at New Westminster.

Others went into industry or went farming. R. B. McMicking left the telegraph and eventually established the beginnings of what became B. C. Hydro in Victoria with a street lighting plant. R. H. Alexander went to the Hastings Mills on Burrard Inlet and as an alderman became an "inviolate part of Vancouver." William Fortune farmed at Tranquille, and A. L. Fortune at Fortune's Landing, an early name for Enderby. J. A. Mara also went farming, but was speaker of the House while a Member of the Legislative Assembly. The Schuberts, who had followed the Thompson, went to the North Okanagan too, and Mrs. Schubert has become the subject of a folk ballad.

CHAPTER SIX

General Growth of Quesnel, 1859-1958

Gold had been found. The region had been established. The government officials had been wrong: neither Quesnel Forks, nor Antler, nor Van Winkle, nor even Richfield, developed as had been predicted. Lt. H. S. Palmer saw them as they really were, small clusters of wooden houses that would remain as packing termini, the cramped natures of their localities preventing their ever becoming towns of any size. The miners had taken possession of the rivers and creeks, the Fraser, the Quesnel, Keithley; they had swarmed over Grouse, Swamp, Antler, Cunningham, Lowhee, Williams, Lightning, down Van Winkle, down the Swift and the Cottonwood. Still no really good site for a town had been found. Barkerville was the best, but when the road was finished, when it was something more than a trail strewn with the carcasses of animals which had died in the attempt to carry goods into the mines, when the circle was almost complete—Cottonwood is only twenty miles from Quesnel— the real centre of Cariboo came to be the junction of the Quesnel and Fraser rivers. Mackenzie had seen the Indians camped there; Fraser had described its beauty and given it a name; the Chinese who followed Ben MacDonald, the first miner at this point, located there. Exploration and furs brought the first passers-by; gold brought the nucleus of a city.

Ben MacDonald's group was followed quickly by hordes ascending the Quesnel River. The first summer was busy: profiteers appeared, and by the spring of 1860 pack trains arrived at the mouth of the Quesnel. In May that year possibly 1,500 men worked the river. Flour cost $1.25 a pound and bacon $1.50. No tools could be bought. The prices at Alexandria were slightly less, but many people went to Cayoosh, as Lillooet was known, for supplies. As white men pressed on farther, the Chinese moved onto the vacated bars, and because the Chinese could obtain little credit farther south, the first store appeared at Quesnel as early as May; a second one, farther up the river, by June. These stores were to supply miners generally, but more particularly the Chinese miners, nearly 500 of whom arrived within the next two years. A gambling tent had been pitched even before the second store. Charles Danielson, immediately following MacDonald, settled at the junction of the rivers instead of going to the mines: pasture was good, and he kept some cattle for butchering.

The following year, 1861, there were two stores at the mouth of the Quesnel and suggestions that the area might itself have gold. Rich Bar Ditch was paying well at the mouth and there was room for another 300 men; just below the mouth, Cornish Bar was yielding six pounds of gold each week. There were some indications that a good-sized town must develop somewhere. Danielson had made money growing turnips which he sold to vegetable-hungry miners and with the profits was building a ferry across the Quesnel River. People thought him foolish because the trip to the mines was made from Williams Lake, where the post office and government agent were located, by Beaver Lake, Quesnel Forks, Keithley and Antler. The mouth of the Quesnel was isolated and off the beaten track; why should a town exist at the mouth of a river where comparatively little gold was to be found?

Yet the government of the day saw fit to reserve land at the junction of the two rivers. One must not underestimate the foresight of the Colonial government: at every site where a town could possibly develop the government reserved ground, and later, if necessary, surveyed it and sold the lots. Alexandria, Quesnel Forks and all the others had been reserved, although not all had been surveyed because, as Moody knew, some were merely "fairs." On May 22, 1862, a public notice appeared in the *Victoria Colonist* reserving lands: "Around the junction of the Quesnelle and Fraser Rivers, extending for a distance of two miles above and two miles below the said junction and to a distance of a half a mile back from the banks of the River Fraser.''

The government was not too soon with its reservations; even at that early date someone had to be hurt. A letter to Col. Moody states that D. McBride had recorded a ranch at this point, had bought plows, teams and other equipment at a cost of $4,000 and now the government had reserved his lands for a townsite! On the 30th of August that year only twenty people were at the mouth of the Quesnel. Twelve days later, at 2.25 p.m., Thursday, September 11, 1862, the Overlanders arrived, beaten, harried, their ranks depleted, headed for the gold fields.

If one must choose the time when Quesnel really began, 1863 would be the best date, though even then it did not have a permanent name: it was known interchangeably as Quesnelle, Quesnelmouth, Quesnellemouth, or Mouth of Quesnel. The road was to be built, and Lt. Palmer had shown that a highway from Quesnel Forks— from where the two branches of the Quesnel River came together to form the main river—to Antler and Richfield would be almost impossible to construct. The best route would be north through Alexandria, thence by boat to Quesnel, along the Cottonwood and into the mines by way of Beaver Pass. At once Quesnelmouth assumed importance as a future distribution and trans-shipment centre. In the spring the *Colonist* reported on the settlement:

> At the mouth of Quesnel there is a town springing up which bids fair to be the largest interior town in B.C. The entire business of the present routes and of the projected coast routes, must eventually centre there....a dozen buildings were in the process of erection ...and the machinery for a sawmill is on the way from Lillooet....

Sensing the importance of rerouting the roads to this place, Colonel Moody lost no time in having the reserved land surveyed and sent Sgt. William McColl to lay out the town in blocks and then in detail. The dozen buildings had been built, sure enough, and many more along the margin of the river, leaving a space too narrow for a street. As a consequence, trouble arose over the laying out of the lots. The work had to be done quickly because many people were anxious to secure property at the anticipated terminal. McColl saw the need for three townsites, Upper, Middle and Lower, and laid off the lots one by two chains in size. The work took him from June 3 to June 22, 1863. Lot 1, Block IV, sold at the first sale of lots at Quesnellemouth on August 17, for £82.

The miniature settlement was approached by "7 miles of execrable, muddy trail." Two ferries were running, the one at the river mouth owned by Danielson, the one three miles up-stream owned by Cook. Hundreds of Chinese were working Nine Mile Bar, and Rich Bar was still prosperous. G. B. Wright was building stables to make a terminus for his winter freight sleighs running to Cottonwood, and Jerome Harper's mill was under construction. The little village had its first serious fire when the woods caught at the mouth of the river; in a high wind, the town had a narrow escape. The future held promises of some international importance: that a telegraph line would pass through Quesnel had been rumoured. When winter came the *Colonist* once more reported on the settlement:

> Mouth of Quesnelle. What a change! The few scattered huts and shanties that in the month of June last collectively struggled for a name—to call it a town or hamlet would be a libel on the language —have all disappeared and are replaced by excellent buildings, fronting on a good street. Everything looks clean, orderly and businesslike. Messrs. Brown and McBride, G. B. Wright, Laumeister and May have control of the business of this future entrepot of the mines. The Steamer ENTERPRISE has been a great success this year. Captain Doane, her commander, is a universal favorite with all classes and creeds.

The collection of houses grew. As roads developed, as shipping on the river increased, more miners sought the New Eldorado. For the first two or three years Quesnel was so much a centre of importance that one newspaper predicted that it would almost certainly be the capital of the confederated colony. Vancouver Island was not reaping the benefits of the gold strikes on the mainland for miners had other ways of entering the mainland colony than through Victoria and the new area was expanding with a population that took money to San Francisco rather than to the Island colony and Victoria. Consequently, the merchants of Victoria favoured union of the two colonies in order that Victoria could be part of the rich area and could, perhaps, control it. Quesnellemouth, as the "stop cock" on the flow of goods to the mines, was a place to watch.

In 1864 the village received untold publicity when Judge Begbie tried the Indians accused of the Waddington massacres and sentenced five of them to death. The Indian bodies were buried behind a later hospital site. The hanging was of interest to many people: government officials worried about the repercussions of this hanging on other Indians of Chilcotin, but to the people of Cariboo the hanging was an excuse for a celebration, and miners of the district congregated at Quesnel for the "party." One couple, William and Lizette Boucher, had had no real honeymoon after their wedding at St. Joseph's Mission, near Williams Lake, and travelled up from there for the occasion. He was originally a courier for the Hudson's Bay Company, the son of J. G. "Waccan" Boucher who had been with Fraser in 1808. "Billy" Boucher was stationed at Fort Alexandria and in 1864 married Lizette Allard who had been born at Fort George in 1842. He later pre-empted land opposite the town of Quesnel and their son Edward was the first child born there. Mr. Boucher, after whom Bouchie Lake is named, died in 1924; Mrs. Boucher, in 1937.

In 1865 the hundred white people and the hundred "Celestials" living at the junction of the rivers had but one main thoroughfare with all houses facing the Fraser River, none having been built on the narrow, western, river side of the street. Nothwithstanding its fine location the town had improved little since the previous fall. There were hotels, trading posts and restaurants, all of which had barrooms. The Occidental Hotel, the most renowned house and bar on the road to Cariboo, was operated by Thomas Brown and Hugh Gillis, two scions of Great Britain with interests in farming, mining and general trading. One of the trading posts was owned by M. P. Elmore whose daughter Suzie, the second child born in Quesnel— in 1866—married August Baker, an Alsation, who after arriving in Canada had changed his name from Boulanger to Baker. One of the restaurants was run by Chinese, another by "coloured" people. There was a shoemaker, a brewery owned by James Kerr and James Duhig, a drugstore operated by an ancient Chinese apothecary who passed out his own peculiar prescriptions, a livery stable owned by Pollack, two blacksmith shops, and two butcher shops, one of which was run by Russians, who were called "the Mongolians" by local people. The town also had a sawmill, a post office, an express office, a barbershop with bath house, and later a telegraph office.

The coming of the telegraph to Quesnel was an occasion for rejoicing for the little village, but one later of heartbreak for many other people. In 1837 Morse patented the electro-magnet and soon telegraph lines were stretching across continents. An attempt was made in 1857 to lay cable across the Atlantic, but the line broke at a depth of 2,000 fathoms. In 1858 cable was laid from Ireland to Newfoundland, but after three months of operation that one broke too. About this time Perry MacDonough Collins, an American, conceived the idea of linking North America and Europe by a line from Chicago, through British Columbia, across the Bering Sea and through Siberia. After the Western Union Telegraph built as far as San Francisco, Collins interested that company in his plan and sold the negotiations he had made with the United States and Russian governments. In January 1865 the Legislative Council of British Columbia granted Collins permission to string line through the colony, and on March 21st crews laid cable across the Fraser River from New Westminster. The line reached Hope on August 18th and Yale eight days later. Edmund Conway was responsible for the route and on hearing that another Atlantic cable had failed, he doubled his efforts, going up the river, through Soda Creek, Alexandria, to Quesnellemouth. The line was completed to Quesnel at 3 p.m. on September 14, 1865.

That winter Conway had six men at Quesnel building five batteaux capable of carrying four tons each. The following year work continued northward and in a letter to Col. Charles Bulkley, Engineer-in-Chief of the project, and after whom the Bulkley Valley was named, Edmund Conway wrote an account of some of the work they had done in 1866:

> We constructed the Telegraph Road, and line to latitude 55.42 N and longitude 128.15 W. The distance from Quesnel, by the road, is computed at 440 miles, and by the wire 378 miles. There are 15 stations built, a log house, with chimney, door and windows, 25 miles apart. We built bridges over all small streams, that were not fordable, corduroyed swamps. All hill-sides too steep for animals to travel over, were graded, from 3 to five feet wide. The average width of clearing the woods for the wire, is, in standing timber, 20 feet; and in fallen timber, 12 feet. All underbrush and small timber is cleared to the ground, thus leaving the road fit for horses, travelling at the rate of, from 30 to 50 miles per day. Double wires are stretched across all large rivers. Numbes of poles put up 9246. Boats are built for crossing the Bulkley and Westroad rivers.

On July 27, 1866 the steamship *Great Eastern* entered Heart's Content, Newfoundland, carrying cable extending from Ireland. Her arrival spelled doom for the Collins Overland Telegraph, although those connected with it hoped this latest attempt to cross the Atlantic would also end in failure. It did not. Slowly Collins's plans were abandoned: the line was left strung along the route, heavy equipment was stored in a blockhouse build at Fort Stager especially for this purpose and guarded there by John McCutcheon until 1869. Indians fell heir to the equipment left along the roadway. Indians fell heir to the wire too, and from it made fish traps and baskets as well as repairs to their famous suspension bridges across the rivers. Civilization was at last affecting the most northerly tribes.

To Quesnel, the line, completed or not, was a boon, for it remained in action to that point, and in 1868 was extended to Barkerville. In February 1871 the British Columbia government took over the line from Western Union, and in July of that year turned it over to the Federal government as a fulfillment of one of the terms of Confederation. Eventually, in 1902, the old line beyond Quesnel was re-opened and completed to the Yukon.

With improved communication both by telegraph and road, the town moved steadily forward. News travelled more quickly and reports of other gold rushes reached the town by wire. As the men poured through to new fields or returned to more familiar ones, new stores and businesses appeared, only to close as the trade died again. The great Cariboo Gold Rush was over by 1865 and although a great flow of gold continued to leave the Williams Creek area, most towns became smaller and smaller.

Quesnel, however, continued to prosper. As mines failed on Williams Creek, or demanded greater amounts of capital for working, returning miners passed through Quesnel. In 1868 H. F. "Twelve-Foot" Davis, the man who had taken $15,000 from a 12-foot strip between the Little Diller and the Abbott claims on upper Williams Creek, had found Arctic Creek. Michael Burns and Vital La Force then wintered on the headwaters of the Omineca and returned to Quesnel, spreading news of great wealth in the north. With backing from the government, an expedition, headed by Burns, went north in May but returned with unfavourable reports, a contradiction of their first intimations. The party was followed

and overtaken when it again went northward from Quesnel, and
Burns and his group were forced to admit that they had discovered
a new creek and had taken $8,000 from it in thirty-five days. They
agreed then to lead the newcomers into the area on condition that
the discoveres could stake first. Burns led them to Vital Creek, a
tributary of the Omineca. Another rush was on.

Goods sent by the interior route passed through Quesnel to
Fort St. James, Taché and Middle rivers, to Takla Lake and into
Vital, Manson and Germanson creeks. In 1871 the excitement
reached its peak and by the middle of June Rufus Sylvester, the
expressman at Quesnel, said that already 800 animals, mostly laden
with provisions, had crossed the Fraser at that point and had passed
over the road built by G. B. Wright to the Blackwater country, but
mapped originally by Edmund Conway.

Quesnel remained the base of supplies, although the new mines
were 230 miles northward, and Quesnel merchants kept prices as
low as possible. In fact, prices in Omineca were never so high as
they had been in the early days of Cariboo because merchants realized
that these miners would pass that way again. Better to make two
fair profits than only one exorbitant one.

Omineca played out. Fortunately Cassiar was discovered in
1874, but it too had seen its best days by 1876. Quesnel, as distributing point, was saved again, for by this time further discoveries
had been made on Lightning Creek, and hydraulic operations had
come into use on Williams Creek. In the meantime British Columbia had entered Confederation to become a Canadian Province, but
the western colony had made certain demands. Canada needed the
west with its fortunes and was willing to supply conveniences,
including the Canadian Pacific Railway, in order to acquire them.
The western colony wanted connections with the east and preferred
to unite with Canada, basically a British area, rather than its alter-
native choice, the United States.

Quesnellemouth became "Quesnelle" for post office purposes,
and shortly afterward businesses increased in number. By 1882 there
were two hotels, the most important being the Occidental, by that
time owned by John McLean; four merchants and trader's stores—
Reid and Hibbard, the Hudson's Bay Company, Abraham Barlow,
and T. De Nouvion, and three Chinese stores—Kwong Lee and
Company, Wah Lee, Yan War. Ti Loy had a bakery; Alfred Car-

son and Robert Middleton were blacksmiths; M. P. Elmore, his brother George, and "Twelve Foot" Davis traded in furs, while Charles August did the local carpentry. A school was soon established but was closed after three months because of a shortage of pupils.

Population was largely transient; for years, between excitements, the town never really grew in size. Some changes were made, but "the 100 whites and 100 Celestials" did not vary much in number although they may have done in character. The *British Columbia Directory* for 1885 lists fifty-one people receiving mail at Quesnel Post Office, and two years later lists only seven additional names. Alexandria was as large as Quesnel or Keithley. Barkerville, however, had many times the number of people. Unsuccessful gold miners went trapping during the winter months and sold furs to the Hudson's Bay Company at Quesnel, which became one of the most important fur depots.

The next rush northward was to Klondike and Yukon, and the interior route divided at Quesnel. The road across the river, the route travelled by the men headed for Manson Creek, was again in use and swung west to cross the Skeena at the Sestoot, and there it met the Old Trail to Telegraph Creek on the Stikine. The other trail turned towards Cottonwood, down the Willow River to Giscombe Portage and on to Fort McLeod, following the route Mackenzie should have used a hundred years earlier. This course met the Black and Dease rivers and the Old Trail at Fort Selkirk.

The interior route, as opposed to the one by way of Skagway, was not very important for this rush to the latest Eldorado, although Quesnel did get some trade. Travellers passed through, buying at one of the stores, staying a night at a hotel, drinking at the saloons and having one last look at a semblance of civilization before turning into the wilds. Many of course did not stop. They may have stepped off the stage when it halted in front of James Reid's store, taken the ferry across the Fraser, and set off immediately to seek their fortunes without having glanced at the village of false fronts.

The eight years before World War I was a period of railway boom in Canada, and the entire country became real estate conscious. With the building of the Grand Trunk Pacific, Prince George came into the "lime light" along with numerous smaller places to the west which, if one judges from promoters' advertisements, were all destined to become great cities within a very short time. Although on the outskirts of this surge of interest to the north, Quesnel was in the mainstream of early traffic. People once more travelled the old telegraph trail, this time in search of farm land that could be producing by the time a railway was constructed. At one time hopes were high that the Grand Trunk Pacific would follow the Fraser south to Vancouver, but instead, and to the great disappointment of the settlement at the mouth of the Quesnel, the line went to Prince Rupert. By that time, of course, the dreams were of another railroad.

This railway building period was another of expansion for Quesnel and gave the hamlet form, both physical and social. Thousands of people moving to newly advertised areas near Vanderhoof and Smithers and Fort St. James went to Quesnel. Some went no farther, but instead remained in the valleys that come under the influence of the town: Nazko, Narcosli, Dragon, Bouchie, Macalister. At this time the hamlet acquired a newspaper, and fraternal organizations.

The railway boom that brought the sleeping Fort George to life was also responsible for the concept of the Pacific Great Eastern Railway. In 1912 construction of this line was commenced, to connect Vancouver with Prince George where it was to join the Grand Trunk Pacific, proceed to the Peace River country and beyond to the Rockies, through Pine Pass to the Alberta boundary 380 miles from Quesnel. Since the completion of the Canadian Pacific, the closest railroad had been at Ashcroft, but a north-to-south line had to be built in order to tap the British Columbia hinterland. When the contractors, Foley, Welsh and Stewart, failed and then dropped their contract, the British Columbia government became the owner of the line and opened it from Squamish to Clinton. From there construction begain in order to fulfill the original intentions.

In October 1921 the first train ran from Squamish to Quesnel. The railroad did not reach Prince George until October 1952, and did not run from Squamish to Vancouver until 1956. For decades the railroad was known as the one that "started no where and ended no where"; it was the "Please Go Easy," the "Province's Greatest Expense." British Columbia's railway was, in most circles, considered to be a failure. It did not bring the expected 258,000 new settlers. It was slow. It was rickety. It was the butt of every hoary old railway joke ever told. But the Pacific Great Eastern was a new artery to the north, and until its arrival at Quesnel the interest in quartz mining had not arisen. The coming of the railway gave quartz mining prospectors the opportunity to introduce heavy equipment. In the 1920s, papers carried news of Blair and Tregillus at Proserpine Mountain, of the Hixon Hills, of coal and oil at Australian, of scheelite on Hardscrabble Mountain, of diatomite deposits and even of platinum.

By 1927 the town had recovered from the post-war depression. Because of the interest in quartz, in the still-hoped-for-dreams of the completed railway, and in hydraulic and placer mining, Quesnel rode the wave of prosperity with the rest of the world. Local affairs had been managed by the Board of Trade since its formation in 1910, but at this time the area felt that it was not receiving just returns on its provincial taxes and that it would thrive better if incorporated as a village entitled to manage its own affairs. In March 1928, the *British Columbia Gazette* showed Quesnel and North Quesnel united as the Municipality of the Village of Quesnel.

As early as 1928 old Barkerville was again astir and talking boom, but one reporter said that the old town had ''a good barber and a shoemaker but both are dead—hardly a live asset.'' Both were buried in the old, rundown Williams Creek cemetery.

When the depression hit Quesnel the government tried to direct men towards the land as settlers, but the country was overrun by unemployed who read in coast papers of huge amounts of gold being taken from the great river. In fact, it appeared to be a conspiracy among coast newspapers to start a small rush to rid the big cities of the unemployed. The story is told, however, of two tired and dead-broke prospectors who arrived in Quesnel. One sold his rifle to tide them over, but by the Labour Day race meet the money was nearly finished and they decided to try their luck with what was left. On Monday they made $100; on Tuesday they picked four winners. They bought a grubstake, built a boat, and went down the Fraser to a bar which proved to be good. That winter they spent in Quesnel and saved enough money to start again in the spring.

Such men were available for work when Fred M. Wells's Cow Mountain precipitated the orgy of snow-staking in the winter of 1932–33. Island Mountain on Jack of Clubs Lake, four and a half miles west of old Barkerville, was the focal point of the Second Cariboo Gold Rush. The new rush in quartz required more money; only large, wealthy organizations could bring in the necessary machinery. Nevertheless, the new rush brought its interesting people, and stories about "The Lucky Swede" will be as interesting in later years as those of Cameron, Evans, Barker and Willoughby are today.

But organization was more apparent in the growth of the new, rich fields. The planned town of Wells was laid out in December 1933. It was a modern mining town that grew quickly, efficiently, and in an orderly manner, and with all the conveniences of a large city. The town was wheelshaped, with the hub on top of a knoll; churches, stores, banks, theatres, hospital, newspaper, and recreational centres, were located on the "spokes" and "rim." In 1933, at the depth of the depression when, as Roderick MacKenzie, M.L.A. for Cariboo, said, gold was "the brightest thing in British Columbia," the lure of gold, as it had seventy years earlier, attracted all types of people, including those who tried to take it away from the ones who had acquired it by hard work. Like Williams Creek of old, Jack of Clubs Lake attracted its share of bootleggers, gamblers and sharpies, as well as the solid citizens required to promote a lasting community.

Once again, though not so slowly this time, the mouth of the Quesnel River assumed importance as the "stop cock," the distributing centre for the mines. The year 1932 was the best since 1910: $9,000 worth of lots were sold; $55,000 worth of new buildings erected, and $550 was paid into the treasury for trade licences. The following year the amount paid for licences rose to $937, collected from 105 businesses. New tradesmen and new farmers appeared, new industries to serve Wells, the gold town "57 miles and 788 curves away." The quartz boom solved the depression problem for Quesnel and Wells, and predictions for placer work in the area were enthusiastic. The boom attracted world-wide interest. As early as June 1933 F. Grayman of New York and N. Laptev of the U.S.S.R. arrived in Quesnel on their way to the mines where Laptev wanted to make a study of methods of placer and lode mining. He was employed by the Soviet government in developing gold-rich lode and placer properties in Russia.

War came again. Government policy and general attitudes towards gold mining ended the first phase of the Second Cariboo Gold Rush. The Jack of Clubs Lake settlement all but disappeared. Wells almost became a ghost town when labour was at a minimum and the Cariboo Gold Quartz company could hire no workers for gold mining. The government freezing order dealt the mines a final blow which was felt by July 1942. The next year Cariboo-Hudson went up for sale, a casualty of war. Following the peace, other problems arose in the region. At Wingdam, first operated in 1897, a company failed to defeat the old slum troubles. By 1946, however, Cariboo Gold Quartz was able to hire more men, and the discovery of rich gold ore veins made by the company brought the old Lowhee area to the fore once again. Strikes, however, caused a slow start, though some impetus was given mining by the rise in the price of gold from $25 to $42 on excess of production between July 1, 1946 and June 30, 1947.

The war brought both financial and social ruin to Wells, but Quesnel still prospered. The old town had had reverses in the past, but was adaptable. For years the great forests of the coast had been mercilessly cut while logging and lumbering in the interior had been developed only for local purposes. The war brought about a change. Britain, in her search for a high-speed, manoeuvrable, cheap fighter-bomber, had developed the Mosquito, the fastest in the world and it was made of plywood. Ideal for these laminated aircraft, Quesnel birch was fairly free of knots and could be glued effectively. It was cut, shipped to New Westminster, processed, and sent to Britain. Promoters then began taking an interest in the Cariboo forests, and by 1947 the pit-prop industry was making a good beginning with pit-props going directly to Britain for use in the Welsh coal mines. Horsefly supplied cedar telephone poles. Sawmills began to appear between Soda Creek and Strathnaver. In 1946 there were 33 sawmills in the district; in 1951 there were 147; in 1958, over 100 sawmills and 11 planer mills. Talk of plywood and pulp factories began; the coast was at last awakening to the value of the Cariboo woods. Lack of transportation, industry and general isolation had curtailed the full growth of Quesnel lumbering. Transportation always has been, is, and always will be, the key to the development of Quesnel and the area it services.

CHAPTER SEVEN

Commercial Growth of Quesnel

Quesnel began in 1863; the region was established. Roads crossed the Quesnel River at its mouth; businesses started to appear. Hotels were built; banks were necessary. Before too long, churches, schools and hospitals, a newspaper, fraternal orders and some amusements were established and, in time, expanded to make the town what it is today.

Trade and commerce came into the district long before the gold rush. The Hudson's Bay Company had been trading with the Indians since 1821 and the North West Company before that. In exchange for furs the Company kept the Indians supplied with goods, and by keeping the Indian in debt the Company was assured of trade. The forts stocked only goods which would be purchased by the natives or by its own employees. After Peter Dunlevy broke this rule and obtained mining supplies from Kamloops, the country was soon overrun by gold seekers and the great firm carried miners' supplies, but sold these supplies at a very high price. In time the mining town had their own stores, the steamer by-passed Alexandria en route from Soda Creek to Quesnel, and the road built to the mining towns had their own stores, the steamer by-passed Alexandria therefore, saw no further need for a store at Alexandria. Business had been decreasing there as early as 1863 while Manson was in charge, and in June 1867 the old fort closed. Alexandria became only a farm to supply the district and was leased the following year to Archibald Mackinlay of Lac La Hache. The store at Quesnel opened in September 1866 to recoup losses sustained at Alexandria, with Hugh Ross in charge. Employees, company-trained men now unemployed, and knowing how much the Company had made, started their own businesses, and stores appeared in many localities.

In the meantime, other people had moved into the Upper Fraser area to trade. According to the *Colonist* of September 30, 1859 "a man named Palmer came down with 680 oz. of gold dust or $11,500" from the sale of goods taken up-river by pack mule in April. Palmer did not go as far north as Quesnel, but others did. The next year hundreds of pack animals carried goods to the north. Nothing but an Indian village stood at the mouth of the Quesnel when Ben MacDonald panned the first yellow sand, but in May of the following year there was a small log store. When Philip Henry Nind, a government official, arrived there a year later, in 1861, two stores supplied the Chinese, who had taken over the bars vacated when the Occidentals moved farther up the Quesnel River. In 1862 the Overlanders arrived to find one store run by a Mr. Whitehall who was charging $1.50 for a meal. Whitehall later left the grocery business and, with Draper, discovered the wealth of Cunningham Creek in 1864. His store was taken over by a Mr. Dodge who had employed W. C. King, a man who later took an active part at the Yale Convention of 1868, the convention to decide whether or not British Columbia should join the Dominion of Canada.

The surveying of the townsite in 1863 and the knowledge that the road was going through the junction settlement were the cues for the storekeepers to move into this section. Thomas Brown and Donald McBride built close to the wharf which had been constructed for the steamer *Enterprise*. Frank Laumeister, almost broke after his unsuccessful attempt to use camels on the new road, opened a supply depot for the miners. Livery stables and blacksmith shops mushroomed. The sawmill was erected at the foot of Front Street; a carpenter, a barber, and a druggist began doing business in the riverfront community. The following year, in the spring of 1864, Barnard's Express and the Bank of British Columbia opened buildings facing the river, south of Carson Avenue next to what became Hudson's Bay Company Corner. That same year showed indications that placer mining was ending for the small operator: by fall the exodus was so great that merchants were complaining of hard times. No new stores came for some years.

The Hudson's Bay Company store opened in Barkerville in 1867 with John M. Work in charge. At Quesnel, the Company first rented buildings in 1866 but in 1867 built two warehouses, a dwelling and a store, all of them of log. The store faced the river on the corner of what are now Front Street and Carson Avenue and the warehouses were on Carson and Reid Street. Between the two was the dwelling house for Factor Graham who operated the business. Robert Williams was in the Quesnel store for many years after Graham; he was replaced by R. J. Skinner who took a leading part in the life of the town, socially, economically and politically.

The year 1915 was a hard one for Cariboo, and the Hudson's Bay Company, as well as its opposition, was affected. The Prince George branch was forced to close, although the one in Quesnel remained open another four years: the *Cariboo Observer* of May 24, 1919 sadly related that the Quesnel store was closing. As a memento of its long stay in Cariboo, the Company left the last canoe that carried freight from Fort St. James to Quesnel by way of the Stuart, Nechako and Fraser rivers. Made from a cottonwood log, it was 50 feet long, 4½ feet wide and 3 feet deep, and capable of carrying 5 tons. The canoe remained on the river bank across Front Street from the old store building until it rotted and was removed. The building was purchased by C. H. Allison, who used it for his drugstore and the post office. The post office was located there until another building was rented, and it remained in the rented one until November 1953 when space was ready in the new federal building. A. J. Elliott bought the warehouse on the corner of Reid Street and Carson Avenue.

By the end of 1865 Kwong Lee and Company, formerly in mining with "Billy" Ballou on Ferguson's Bar but with mercantile interests in Victoria and Barkerville, had acquired a store on Barlow Avenue. P.L. Johnson was running the Colonial Restaurant, and the Central Cafe was booming. This last landmark was torn down in 1935 and a service station was built on the site. An old barn which stood on Front Street next to the Cariboo Hotel for many years was moved to the back of the lot in 1935 and demolished by Harold Cleland in 1937.

The telegraph trail opened a new route through Quesnel, and by 1867 the village was an important centre of trade for another district. Stores opened to serve people going to Peace River, but closed when that rush faded. At that time the Wah Lee Company opened, operating on Barlow Avenue until 1939, though great-grandsons of Wah Lee carry on the business under the name Keen's. Kwong Foo, who came to Cariboo in 1869 at the age of twenty-four and worked for Wah Lee for a short while, was one of the many interesting Chinese figures in town. In later years he lived at the Nam Sing ranch, four miles from Quesnel, and died there in 1943. Yan War also opened his store on Front Street and Barlow Avenue in 1869.

In 1873 James Reid turned from prospecting to trading. With Hibbard Hudson he built the largest and most completely stocked store in the region on the corner of Front and Carson. Reid soon became the leading personality in the district, building steamers, owning flour and saw mills, backing Hixon Creek Mines, and controlling numerous other enterprises. He became a Member of Parliament in 1881 and served in that capacity until 1888 when he was made Senator, a position he occupied for sixteen years until his death in 1904. After Senator Reid died, the store was managed by John Anderson Fraser, who had come to Quesnel to teach school but had resigned his position to work in the general merchandise business. Fraser bought and opened his own store in 1909 and generally took over the community leadership relinquished by Reid. The business was incorporated in 1912 as a Joint Stock Company. Fraser became school trustee, promoter of a brewery, mining magnate, and eventually a political leader.

Reid's chief opposition had come from the Hudson's Bay Company and from a store owned by M. P. Elmore, who was wiped out by fire in December 1874 and turned to fur trading and to running a pack train to Summit Lake. No other opposition appeared until Telesphore Marion opened in 1894 to deal primarily with the Indians and to ship furs directly to England. By 1900 he was able to build the sternwheeler *Quesnel*. He brought the first gramophone to the settlement and in 1915 owned one of the first automobiles. The first garage in Quesnel was built by Albert Boyd who had been born at Cottonwood. George Johnston had started a livery stable in Quesnel after the Reid estate mill closed, and before he died in 1954 had developed his business into a garage with his showroom on the site of the first blacksmith shop.

These stores were the basic ones; others came and flourished as the town grew. C. D. Hoy, Reginald Boothe, W. T. Ewing, J. Cowan, Overwaitea, S. N. Williams established themselves, and in 1949 Roderick Mackenzie of Williams Lake planned to enlarge his chain of stores which had branches at Squamish, Williams Lake and Wells, but only opened a men's furnishing store.

Following the general growth of the mining district, banking companies began to build branches where needed. In early days of Cariboo banks were of little economic importance, for nuggets were the medium of exchange and banking houses were used only as storage vaults. Miners did not sell or deposit gold with the branches, preferring to ship the dust to San Francisco themselves where they received from two to three dollars more an ounce for it.

MacDonald's, a private Victoria banking concern, opened a branch on Williams Creek in 1863 with a Mr. Crocker in charge, but closed within a year. Russell of the Bank of British Columbia, a bank backed by British money, opened at Richfield the same year, moved to Camerontown, and to Barkerville two years later when business became concentrated at that point. The British Columbia Savings Bank of Cariboo, in Barkerville, did not last long; it had only 53 deposits in 1870 and fewer in 1871. Meanwhile, the Bank of British North America opened at Richfield in 1865 and the next year moved to Barkerville with Robert Merrill as manager. These last two banks closed in 1872. Walter Young, manager of the Camerontown branch of the Bank of British Columbia, left a description of it:

> At Camerontown, the office was a two-roomed shack, built of boards, and with many a chink through which the snow used to drift, until the walls were lined with cotton and paper. The safe was simply an iron box about three feet by two, and two and a half feet high. It had a lid with only one lock and no combination, and was often so full that there was difficulty in getting the lid to close.

At Quesnel, the Bank of British Columbia opened an office on Front Street between Barnard's Express office and the Hudson's Bay Company store, with Walter Young as manager. The banking company knew that life was rugged in mining areas where living costs were high—board was $25 a week in Quesnel—and he gave employees a "goldfield allowance" which amounted to $125 in Barkerville and $100 a month in Quesnel. The men slept in the bank.

> The bank building [Young noted] was a log house with a lot of bear skins tacked on the outside to dry, the owners of the skins putting them up without even asking permission. We treated our customers well, had a good fire, and furnished plug tobacco free, with a sharpened axe-head and a board to cut it on.

The bank also had a small warehouse in the rear for storing goods on which advances had been made. The great rush over, the branch closed on October 27, 1866. Inhabitants of Quesnel then used Barkerville banks until they too closed their doors. After that the nearest banks were in Ashcroft.

For over forty years Quesnel had no bank, and business was conducted at Ashcroft until 1909 when the Northern Crown Bank opened in Quesnel's Town Hall building. This bank closed in 1917. The Canadian Bank of Commerce, which had absorbed the Bank of British Columbia many years earlier, opened a branch in 1920, and a new branch of the Royal Bank of Canada began operating in 1928.

The social centres of the early town of Quesnel were the hotels. Although many appeared, closed and were never heard of again, hotels were while they lasted business houses of great importance. The Fashion Hotel entertained Governor Seymour while he was on

his trip to the mines. P. L. Johnson, who started in a small way in 1865 with the Colonial Restaurant, expanded his business the following year to open the Colonial Hotel. The restaurant was lost in a fire of 1874 and the hotel was rebuilt, but operated by numerous people over the years. Other hotels, such as the Nugget and Globe, were on a less pretentious scale.

In Quesnel, however, by far the most important hotel was the Occidental which attracted colony-wide attention with its service. The supply store of Thomas Brown and Donald McBride had closed in 1864 and the following year Hugh Gillis and Thomas Brown opened their great hotel on Front Street, on the site of the present Quesnel Hotel. A two-storey building with a double-deck verandah on the front, the Occidental catered to the best class of traveller, but also welcomed local people to use its saloon, dining room, dance hall, display rooms and lavish bedrooms. Hugh Gillis committed suicide in 1871 and Alfred Carson took over his interest. Carson's share was acquired by Brown, who died in May 1881; Sarah Ann, his widow, married John McLean.

McLean had reached the site of Quesnel on June 21, 1859 when the banks and benches of the river were covered with big timbers. Because there were no open spaces, he camped on the bank in front of the site where his Occidental Hotel stood in later years. In 1859 no less than 400 Indians had been camped about the place, most of them on the flats just above town. The hotel site had been an Indian burying ground.

The McLeans operated the hotel until they retired, then rented it to Perkins and Bowron, who kept it a year. It was then rented to William Boyd, son of John Boyd of Cottonwood House. Following him were A. Johnson and A. Hoffencamp, who carried on business for four years until 1907, when Edward L. Kepner bought the old place. He tore the building down in 1910, erected a new three-storey hotel on the original site, and refurbished two older buildings on either side of the Occidental which became known as the North and South annexes. When this new building opened, Kepner threw the key into the river to signify that the hotel would never close.

In 1910, farther along the street but in the same block, John Strand built the Cariboo Hotel, and Quesnel then had two fine hotels. The fire that burned the business section of town in January 1916 destroyed both of them. John McLean had died the year before, but Mrs. McLean, who did not die until 1920, watched her old property go up in a blaze. Kepner, once a miner, left the hotel business. Strand rebuilt an old hotel, but Quesnel was left without one for some time. William T. Ewing, who had operated a meat market, then bought the building of the defunct North Quesnel Boarding School, which had formerly been operated by the Anglican mission, and set it on concrete at the site of the old Occidental; but Ewing died before it opened as the British-American Hotel. Percy Elsey bought the business and operated it as the New Quesnel Hotel until he sold to J. D. Pearson and R. Laughton in 1933. Pearson's daughter married Arne Hassel-Gren, a later owner. In 1924, J. Pearson had bought the Cariboo Hotel from Strand.

With banks, hotels, stores, a brewery, flour mills and other mercantile pursuits, the old town in time found itself with a medium by which to advertise. The land boom of 1908 brought a newspaper, which was established primarily for the circulation of real estate notices. In September 1908, J. B. Daniell began publication of the *Cariboo Observer*, but in 1910 it was taken over by the Northern Printing Company Limited with Daniell as editor and J. G. Quinn as manager. Within two months Quinn went to Prince George to manage the *Tribune*, and H. L. Stoddard became manager of the *Observer*. Early in 1911 Albert Dollenmayer and John G. Hutchcroft assumed ownership, with Hutchcroft as managing editor. In April of that year the government reserved all land in the area and the newspaper said "The Provincial Government's recent order-in-council stops agricultural development of the Cariboo—as a blow on the head with a club would stun a deer." The land reservation was also a blow for the newspaper, which made its profit from land advertisements. In July Hutchcroft wrote a valedictory editorial, but the paper did not have to cease publication because E. L. Kepner, the hotelman and part owner of the local telephone company, took it over and retained Hutchcroft as editor. After Kepner left town, Hutchcroft became sole owner.

For many years the influential little newspaper backed many beginning community organizations. It encouraged the development of the Board of Trade, the hospital, the Anglican Church, and the travelling library service. When the first automobiles drove into Quesnel, the *Observer* began to call for better roads to serve the agricultural lands and gold areas. The need for a road from the mouth to the forks of the Quesnel River the paper brought to the fore again and again, and as late as 1938 and 1946.

At first the paper was staunchly Conservative in politics, but after 1917, except for backing Louis LeBourdais, it steered clear of political issues. For some years the paper carried Prince George news, but after the *Tribune* was well established there the *Cariboo Observer* paid little attention to its town's northern rival. In later years the same policy was followed with news of Wells and Williams Lake, but whereas the *Observer* carried on a not-too-friendly feud with the town to the north, it has always been on friendly terms with those of the east and south.

Hutchcroft died in 1934 and his son carried on publication until 1949 when the business was taken over by W. L. Griffith who incorporated his *Wells Chronicle* into the *Cariboo Observer* on September 1, 1949. Griffith expanded the business to the extent that in 1950 he was able to print a second section. The following year he installed a new press.

The *Observer* was the only publication in the town for many years, but in January 1945 the *Cariboo Digest* appeared. The name has changed several times since and each change indicates the ever-increasing scope of the publication. It became the *Cariboo and Northern British Columbia Digest, Cariboo and Northwest Digest* and, in July 1951, *Northwest Digest*. Grace Pearl Howlett's "Quesnel Printers" issued the first copy, but in August 1945, Alexander Sahonovitch and Vernon H. Frank became publishers when the Cariboo Digest Limited bought the Howlett business. The company had an authorized capital of $10,000 and the shareholders included names from the small communities of Cariboo, names of people interested in their district. The masthead of the magazine informed its readers that it is the "Official Organ of B.C. Registered Trappers Ass'n." The magazine features articles of interest on transportation, mining, trapping, game preservation, and community history. By 1955 Wesley Logan and Arthur Downs had assumed owernship, but M. Maundrell replaced Logan. The periodical appeared six times each year and although the material was devoted to the northwest of British Columbia, subscriptions went as far as Europe and Malaya.

In 1952 F. W. Lindsay started publication of an ad-journal, the *Quesnel Advertiser*, a jaunty history-conscious weekly.

CHAPTER EIGHT

Social Growth of Quesnel

Social life in Cariboo was highly developed, especially in Barkerville where the mixture of nationalities, creeds and attachments were varied, but prompted a mature development. It reached its peak in Barkerville by the time of the fire in 1868 with fraternal orders, dance halls, gambling rooms, sports and other amusements, as well as a library. On the creeks, prize fights and throwing the stone were popular, especially before women arrived. With the arrival of the ladies—more respectable ladies that is— more formal parties enlivened the evenings of the more respectable men as the various hostesses vied with each other for the title of leader in the social whirl.

In very early times the variety of peoples is evident in celebrations of national and religious days. Christmas was not a big season on the creeks because most miners had left for Quesnel or for the coast, and since those miners who did not leave were usually the destitute; only people in business celebrated traditionally. However, St. Patrick's Day, the Queen's Birthday, St. George's Day and the Day of Atonement were kept appropriately. Before the heavy tariffs were levied on non-British miners, many on the creeks were American and one of the greatest celebrations was Independence Day. By 1867 Cariboo, which had been advocating confederation with Canada for so long, was ready to welcome the birth of the new

Dominion even though far away. After 1871 the First of July was usually noisy both on the creeks and at the mouth of the Quesnel. Williams Creek took on a fairy-land appearance when every window in every house showed a lighted candle at night, and fireworks exploded in the black valley. The first of July was always opened with a speech and with the singing of "God Save the Queen," while the Fourth opened with a speech and "The Star Spangled Banner." Both started at midnight with the booming of salutes simulating those of cannon by detonating miners' caps on blacksmiths' anvils.

At the Mouth of Quesnel the First of July was not celebrated until after 1871, but the Fourth was. Quesnel's horse racing interest goes back to races held on Front Street along the grassy river bank and to the many Americans and Englishmen in the vicinity with racing backgrounds. Pasturage was better at Quesnel than in the mountainous mining area and so there were more horses. The *Cariboo Sentinel* of July 8, 1865 carried news under the heading "Quesnel Races":

> These races came off at the Mouth of Quesnel on the 4th inst. Frank Way's 'Boston Colt' won the 1st race for $200; Johnson's horse 'Bucephalis' the 2nd for $100; the scrub race was won by a horse called 'Dick', beating four others. Messrs. Ball, J.P., and Bates were judges, and Messrs. Duhig, Goudie, and Hunt, the stewards. The day was fine, the attendance large, and the races most exciting.

Race and feast days were not the only times for amusement. Hotel and saloon, "the giddy Court of mirth and revelry" as James Anderson called it, grew rapidly and flourished in Cariboo, where each stopping place was licensed to sell liquor and developed into a recreational centre. Barkerville in 1868 had eighteen saloons and the best of them had a barroom, card-room, and dance hall where hurdy-gurdy girls danced for pay and where weary miners gathered in the brightly lighted halls. At the Mouth of Quesnel, Thomas Brown and Hugh Gillis built their Occidental Hotel. Their dance hall was used for years by the old men of town who drank whiskey neat while playing a friendly game of chequers. But the games were not always so friendly: stud poker and faro flourished to relieve the miner of his poke. When Constable David Anderson of the provincial police in Quesnel received orders to stop all gambling in the bars under a law of 1868, he destroyed an established social custom:

no longer could one even play cards or chequers to see who "paid the shot."

Another important part of Cariboo social life was the library. First established in Camerontown by money collected through subscription and with John Bowron as librarian, it was poorly located, and was moved to Barkerville where the building also housed the post office. Bowron paid for the new building himself, offering to operate the post office and library at a salary of $160 a month without charging rent. The government refused to pay and Bowron was replaced.

Bowron was also a leading participant in local theatricals. Troupes of travelling minstrels passed through from time to time, but more popular was the Cariboo Amateur Dramatic Association which opened the Theatre Royal in May 1868, a building razed in 1937 to make way for a new community hall. The chief playwright on the creek was James Anderson, better known for his "Letters to Sawney."

In this centre, where all types of men gathered, the fraternally minded grouped themselves into societies. The "Caledonian Benevolent Society" was formed in 1867, for example. During the gold rush a great many members of eastern Masonic lodges who had come to the goldfields wanted their own branch, and in 1866 held an organizational meeting of all Masons on Williams Creek. In 1867 dispensation was granted to form Cariboo Lodge No. 469 A.F. & A.M. Oppenheimer and Company constructed a building 20 feet by 40 feet, the lower portion to be used by them and the upper portion as the Masonic Hall. The first hall was destroyed by the fire of 1868, and a new one consecrated in June 1869 was destroyed by fire in December 1936, though rebuilt the following year.

For these first few years the Mouth of Quesnel was a "nobody" —anyone of any importance was at Barkerville. Quesnel was merely a "jumping off" place. Only five families "mattered": the R. J. Skinners, J. Duhigs, A. Barlows, J. St. Laurents and W. A. Johnstons. Though the town at the junction had its horse races and its ice skating and its swimming, and though the hotels, restaurants, saloons and private homes there had their dances and games and other social events, the community attracted little attention. Not until after the Barkerville fire of 1868, after the decline of the more mature and more established mining centre, did Quesnelmouth have a winter social season. When people from the mines moved from the snow and cold of the mountains to a more friendly climate, the village bloomed. Perhaps the first social recognition of Quesnel came from the Barkerville *Sentinel* on February 12, 1875:

> One of the pleasantest events that ever came off in Cariboo came off on the evening of the 10th at Quesnel. I refer to the ball held there and to which invitations were sent over the whole country, from Camerontown to Cache Creek. The Committee were evidently determined to make the affair a success, and it was a success in the fullest sense of the word. By Wednesday evening all had arrived including many from Barkerville, Lightning Creek and Lake La Hache and the ball opened at 9 o'clock p.m. Some sixteen ladies and about twice as many gentlemen were present. Among the former were Mesdames G. Elmore, Duhig, Green, Barlow, Byrnes, Lindsay, Wilson, Boyd, Hyde, Felker, Bowron, and McLeese and the Misses Hyde, Byrnes, Parker, Felkers and Barlow. At 12 midnight the company sat down to a splendid supper and afterwards dancing was resumed and kept up until daylight made the lamp burn dim. On the following evening the ball was again reopened and kept up with even more spirit for by that time everybody knew everybody.... [After another feast] dancing was then recommenced and kept up till 4 o'clock in the morning. On Friday the party broke up and nearly all went home.

As the town grew, other entertainments appeared. Skating, for instance, has always been a Quesnel sport. In time past snow was shovelled from the creeks, or sleighing parties went to Dragon Lake. In 1908, however, a collection was taken in order to build a rink 200 feet by 60 feet near the Reid estate mill: the fence, benches, and work cost $125. Winter sports did not include curling until 1930 when C. H. Allison promoted the rinks and was the first president of the Curling Club. The Quesnel and District Community Centre contains new rinks, and in February 1954 Quesnel won the prized Kelly Cup.

In the summer, like every other town in British Columbia, Quesnel has had its baseball clubs and soft ball clubs. In 1909, near the Court House Lot, the Quesnel Tennis Club grew under the inspiration and direction of Claude Foot. The Golf Club developed in 1930, fostered by banker Colin Malcolm. Lord Willingdon, the Governor-General of Canada and at that time on tour of the country, opened the links and presented a cup. Hunting has always been good in the area, as seen from McLean's notes on Alexandria, but the pheasants have long since vanished. Early gun clubs began enthusiastically and faded from view, though people generally became interested again at Thanksgiving or Christmas turkey shoots. The gun club had been making intermittent efforts to take root, but took on new life in 1930 and has since, as the Rod and Gun Club, been most effective in killing off coarse fish and in planting trout eggs, in addition to passing on to the government a great deal of advice concerning big game management.

Theatricals too have always been popular in the community. The dramatic society received its first impetus in 1910 and has contined ever since, although undergoing many changes in both name and policy. It has, however, steadfastly held to the idea that the legitimate stage is of importance to a Canadian culture, and for this reason Quesnel has been referred to as the "drama city of the interior." In 1946 the group received favourable comment at the Victoria Drama Festival. An offshoot of this club is the Quesnel Arts, formed in 1948 to develop local artistic talent.

Although no group organization promoted moving pictures, the movies have also been popular in Quesnel. The first were brought into the district by a travelling group, but on July 25, 1914 Alexander T. Windt opened his new Rex Theatre with four big reels and music. Windt was exceptionally liberal with his theatre. He removed the seats when anyone wanted to use the building for a dance, and screwed them to the floor again when the dance was over. The building was used for meetings, musical evenings, lectures, travelling musicians and for theatricals, and after the Occidental Hotel was closed to entertaining, the theatre became the community hall. A. J. Elliott, who had ridden a bicycle up the Cariboo road in 1905, took over Windt's interests and, like Windt, cancelled the show for other types of entertainment. The Rex Theatre operated until the new "Carib" was built in 1953.

The community hall is now the Quesnel and District Community Centre. At first it was known as the Quesnel Memorial Arena, but after problems were encountered in financing, building and organizing, a meeting was held in November 1954 in which all local service clubs participated and the name was changed. The Centre is on the lot originally reserved in 1863 as a cemetery. At first the Quesnel War Memorial was to take the form of a lounge and library, but this plan was discarded. In 1950 four or five Quesnel citizens, including Mrs. C. H. Allison, maintained a library in the "Old Log School" while awaiting construction of a new building. The old building has since been removed and the library has been located in the new municipal hall.

Other organizations and fraternal orders appeared or re-appeared. Some have remained active, other have disappeared as members disappeared or transferred to other lodges or clubs. The short-lived Cariboo Club was formed in 1910 to "promote clean good fellowship." The First Cariboo Troop of Boy Scouts was established in 1912 under the leadership of the Rev. W. H. H. Elliott. The Cariboo Brotherhood, the Quesnel Social and Athletic Association, the Bachelors' Club, and the Modern Woodmen of America all started in 1913. In April 1912 resident Masons at Quesnel took steps to form a lodge, but not until September 1913 was Quesnel Lodge Number 269, A.F. & A.M. instituted. George Johnston, whose father had been a member of the old Barkerville lodge, was the first man to join. The new hall opened on October 27, 1934. The Native Sons of Canada became active in 1923. In 1946 Quesnel youth joined with so many others in the Teen Town Movement and elected Glen MacLean first "Mayor." In 1946 the Elks—the B.P.O.E.— was instituted and the Royal Purple Lodge installed the following year. Now the town has branches of most popular service clubs, as well as a Junior Chamber of Commerce.

World War I brought forth patriotic groups and the Great War Veterans' Association formed in 1919 under the aegis of the local land surveyor, E. J. Gook; the following year the Ladies' Auxiliary organized. A war memorial unveiled on September 23, 1922 listed the names of sixty-five Cariboo men who had given their lives for their country. Out of the Great War Veterans' Association grew the Canadian Legion which laid the foundation of the Legion Hall in 1930. Every conceivable method of raising money had to be used but finally shares were sold and the depression conquered; and the great hall opened December 14, 1934. During World War II many groups formed to relieve war distress, one expressly to provide comforts for the men on board the navy vessel *Quesnel.*

Quesnel has had a past, but much of it was lost as the town

grew, as newcomers appeared and as old landmarks were torn down. New information on the town was continually coming to light, but there was no one to preserve it. The Hudson's Bay Company had left a canoe as a reminder of its long stay; the Collins Overland Telegraph had been commemorated by a cairn on the river bank; Lt.-Gov. Randolph Bruce unveiled a Cornish pump which had been donated by W. H. Boyd as a reminder of Quesnel's heritage of gold. But these were only three of the important milestones in Quesnel's long history. In August 1951 William D. Morris interested a group in forming an association to preserve the story of old Cariboo. The group was to encourage and to foster personal histories and worthwhile research about the Cariboo from "Mile 0" at Lillooet to the end of the Barkerville trail. Alvin Johnston became president of this Cariboo Historical Society; George Johnston, Robert Barlow and J. B. Hutchcroft were vice-presidents; Mrs. Sue Speare was secretary and Mrs. J. B. Hutchcroft was treasurer. Their plan was to have a central branch with community organizations in the towns of Cariboo.

CHAPTER NINE

Institutional Growth of Quesnel

Early miners saw the need for a settlement at the mouth of the Quesnel and when the settlement became more established hospitals, schools and churches appeared. At first Quesnel was a pleasant place to spend a winter away from the cold and snow of the mining area, but it was also a place from which the men left as soon as activity began on the creeks once more. Nevertheless, with the establishment of these institutional aspects of social life, more people preferred to remain in Quesnel than to go south to Victoria and San Francisco for the winter.

Probably the first professional surgical operation performed in Cariboo took place in August 1860. Moses Anderson, a renegade from Nicaragua, had been mining on Ferguson's Bar at the mouth of the Quesnel and had shot an Indian boy from the tribal village. Philip Henry Nind, the Justice of the Peace, arrived at Alexandria two days later and after hearing of the affray and foreseeing Indian and miner troubles hastened to the scene of the shooting. Some of the miners had taken compassion on the Indian and had called in Dr. W. B. Wilkinson. When Nind arrived he "found the Indian in a precarious state from a pistol shot wound; the ball had entered his back and lodged in the groin, it had been extracted by Dr. Wilkinson whose skill and attention had under Providence saved the life of the boy."

Many doctors had left the medical profession in search of gold and had gone to Cariboo, the doctor who did this operation at Quesnel being one of them. Others went into the country to practise medicine, but there seems to have been little illness. We know that Dr. F. Trevor went to Quesnel early to practise, but turned to farming when there were not enough sick people in that area to support him . In 1863, however, four doctors were practising on Williams Creek: Drs. Bell, Black, Stephenson and Wabass treated over-packed backs and typhoid, as well as fight and work wounds. Dr. Wabass from Olympia, Washington territory, unfortunately died of rheumatic fever. Two other men died at the same time as the doctor: Edward Tassel of Kent, and Samuel Prager, a Polish Jew who was well known as a packer in British Columbia. The *Colonist* of December 1, 1861 reported that the first birth in Cariboo was the son of a Mrs. John A. Cameron; Mrs. "Cariboo" Cameron died shortly afterwards. Needless to say, had there been a hospital such deaths might have been avoided.

In January 1863 five or six died of smallpox at Quesnellemouth, the bones of one of the victims being uncovered in Quesnel in 1929. When the plague broke out in 1863, a movement began to open a hospital in the mining area. In July of that year, the second Grand Jury, with Judge Begbie in the chair, convened on Williams Creek and requested government aid to build a hospital. The government made a small donation and miners contributed enough that Judge Begbie could lay the foundation log on August 24, 1863 in the presence of the Honourable Donald Fraser, Judge Peter O'Reilly and Thomas Elwyn. In October the building was complete and Dr. A. W. S. Black became first resident surgeon of Cariboo's first hospital. After one year he moved to New Westminster. Dr. Black had come from Australia to the gold fields of California and Cariboo, represented Cariboo West for one session in the Legislative Council, and in 1871 "was found dead on the road" between New Westminster and Burrard Inlet, "having, it appears been thrown from his horse."

For over forty years this Royal Cariboo Hospital was the only one in the region and it operated continuously until 1925. The Wells hospital opened in 1936; it was too small from the outset and the old Barkerville hospital was reconditioned and re-opened but it burned the following year. (The building that burned had been built in 1891 to replace the original of 1863.)

The Royal Cariboo Hospital took patients from all over the area but access was often difficult, especially because of heavy winter roads. Early in 1909 Quesnel decided it needed its own hospital. Great enthusiasm prevailed as the community raised funds by various means, and in 1910 tenders were called to build a hospital on the bank of the Fraser on "One Mile Flat." The hospital board consisted of A. W. Cameron as president and Percy Harrison as secretary-treasurer, with D. H. Anderson, J. L. Hill and the Rev. Stott as committeemen. The *Cariboo Observer* proudly reported that "the plans and specifications as laid down call for a cottage building comprised of a large ward, a private ward, surgeon's room, attendant's room, bath room, kitchen and outhouses."

Mrs. Charlotte Carey, formerly Mrs. James Reid, promised to equip two rooms as a surgery. Six beds were for patients who could obtain hospitalization on a subscription insurance plan for $10 a year. The Ladies' Auxiliary to the hospital was organized in order to raise other money. Mrs. Bohanon, because she was the pioneer lady, was honorary president, and Mrs. W. Ewing was active president. Red Cross days and dances were initiated at once and donations gratefully received.

Almost immediately the new venture met with difficulties. The first nurse resigned before the hospital was opened, and upon opening, the resident physician, Dr. Beech, left. After much trouble in securing a nurse, George Callaghan took the position, but left before Miss Laura Mellefont was hired in the spring of 1911. Her first patient was a horse which had been badly snagged while hauling water from the river.

The following year saw the arrival of Dr. G. F. Baker. He intended to practise there only one year, but remained to become one of the country's most beloved and valued citizens. For years "Doc" Baker travelled by horseback. On one occasion, in freezing winter weather and nourished only on a mixture of condensed milk and Hudson's Bay rum, he rode as far as Barkerville where, within two hours after arrival, he performed the necessary operation. He later acquired a Model T Ford that became well known from Barkerville to Alexis Creek in the Chilcotin, as were his thoroughbreds.

The influenza epidemic of 1918 affected Quesnel and the hospital was overcrowded—any greater catastrophe would have been too much to handle. With the coming of the Pacific Great Eastern Railway, the town expanded and the hospital was in more demand than before. Williams Lake people had no hospital of their own and they too went north on the train for treatment, a small boy once being taken to Quesnel on a speeder. In 1922 collections began once more for a new hospital which was to be opened two years later. In 1936 this one too was crowded and the town appealed to the Provincial government and to the Indian department for help in doubling the accommodation: a new wing 80 feet by 30 feet with ten beds, X-ray and chart rooms were requested. No aid was forthcoming and the board was forced to renovate two wards of the old building. Overcrowding persisted and estimates were called for a new wing costing approximately $12,000. This price did not include the equipment for a maternity ward, four-bed ward, two-bed ward and X-ray room. The money was raised by grants and by hard work on the part of the Ladies' Auxiliary; the wing opened in December 1939.

The war brought increased costs and increased problems. When the Williams Lake hospital closed because it could not obtain a staff, patients from there went north to Quesnel once more. After the war, with incoming pit-proppers and with the expanding lumber industry, even more space was required. Both costs and debts steadily increased and, though $7,500 was donated in the spring of 1947 and more drives for money were initiated, the hospital faced closure. Only the hospital plans instituted by the British Columbia government saved the Quesnel hospital from ruin. A new hospital with ninety beds, the finest equipment and a nurses' residence opened in December 1955 at a cost of almost $900,000, and was named the G. R. Baker Memorial Hospital in memory of Doctor Baker who had done so much for Cariboo.

Like everything else, including medical services, education in Cariboo goes back to the days of the first gold rush when, although there were few children, educated miners occasionally tutored a bright boy or girl. The preachers, too, gave lessons when they could gather enough students. By 1870 the residents along Williams Creek were determined to open a school and everyone appears to have contributed money.

The school building was at first rented, but then one was especially erected and purchased by the people with the aid of a small government grant. The *Cariboo Sentinel* of August 27, 1870 reported that the first teacher, a Miss Clarkson of New Westminster, was expected to arrive the following week. The school was a success, and the following year the government set up a school district with a school board of six. The new teacher, John Mundell, had seven students in this first public school in Cariboo. At the end of March Mundell left, and the school made several efforts to retain teachers, but closed until 1874 when Mrs. Thompson reopened it. The facilities were continued with about sixteen pupils under various teachers until 1905. There were few pupils by that time and although Barkerville had in the past paid higher wages than most towns, it gradually reduced them. Teachers became difficult to hire and the school closed.

Another school district was created in 1877 at Stanley, formerly Van Winkle, then one of the busy centres. Mr. A. Johnstone was the teacher, but within a short time he left and the school closed. Those then desiring an education could go either to Barkerville or else out of the district. In many cases the children of families with means went to Victoria, San Francisco or to Portland, while a few of them went to St. Joseph's Mission at Williams Lake.

At Quesnel, on appeals from the people, the government created a school district on April 14, 1881, but for three years the people could not raise funds either for a school or a teacher. On August 4, 1884 Miss Alice Northcott arrived from Victoria to begin her duties in a log school building that had been rented from the Quesnelle Fire Company and which was located on Front Street next to the present site of the Cariboo Hotel.

The value of the school equipment was $60, and for teaching nineteen boys and ten girls Miss Northcott received $75 a month. The trustees were W. A. Johnston, D. D. Duhig, and Joseph St. Laurent. The school closed soon because of a shortage of pupils, but reopened after three months. Miss N. Dockrill replaced Miss Northcott, but the latter returned in 1888—at a $5 reduction in salary. The trustees were then St. Laurent, Abraham Barlow and J. M. Alexander. The school was not inspected until 1900, but reports were generally favourable: in 1885-86 the first "Honour Rolls" were awarded, to Mary Deschamps for Deportment, Frank Sherman Shepherd for Punctuality and Regularity, and Constance Josephine St. Laurent for Proficiency.

In 1886 the school district name became "Quesnelle" instead

of "Quesnellemouth" and a new school house was built on the present school property. This building was of wood, 16 feet by 24 feet, cost $700, and was on a site 194 by 264 feet which was valued at $60. Eleven years later the lot was reduced in size to 132 by 164 in the hope that a fence could be erected around the smaller property. On Sundays the school was used as a church.

Miss Northcott, who later married Otis Earley, taught until June 1891; in August of that year a young man arrived to take her place. The newcomer was John A. Fraser who taught eighteen pupils until December 31, 1893, when he left teaching to work for James Reid. He was later elected Member of the Legislative Assembly and eventually Member of Parliament for Cariboo. He became a valued school trustee at the same time as Dr. A. D. Morgan in 1903.

In 1900 the name was changed once more, to "Quesnel." Costs of education rose from approximately $50 a pupil to nearly $75. Teachers came and went, some of the women teachers marrying in the community. When in 1906 a school appeared at Soda Creek, with Miss G. Dunlevy receiving $50 a month, Soda Creek children living at Quesnel returned home and the wages at Quesnel were reduced. Mr. Frank Fairey, fresh from Scotland, went to Quesnel to teach in 1908 for the salary of $65, but was given an extra $5 a month to act as janitor. He stayed one year, and subsequently became Deputy Minister of Education for the Province. He retired in 1952, and was later elected to the House of Commons.

Early in 1911 the land boom was in full swing and the town required more teachers. A new two-room log school was built despite the criticism of the *Cariboo Observer* which said the town had outgrown such accommodation, and the old log school was moved along McLean Street to become a private home. Mrs. J. T. Bradey and Miss J. A. Robertson were the teachers. Cariboo was expanding at this time; Alexandria, Barkerville and Dragon Lake opened schools in 1912, and three years later Macalister followed suit. Between 1914 and 1916 the Church of England operated a boarding school and kindergarten for children from outlying area, but because of the war and the growth of rural schools, this was abandoned.

By 1918 Miss Flora Dugan was principal of a Superior School with 124 pupils. In 1921, the first inter-high school sports between

Prince George and Quesnel took place. Prince won the Canadian Rugby event with a score of 70 to 0, but Quesnel won the boys' basketball 22 to 10.

The Second Cariboo Gold Rush made itself felt in the 1930s, and in 1933 Moose Heights opened a school. The townspeople of Quesnel were disgusted by their four school rooms in three separate buildings with "old hard to heat, box stoves in each room." Three years later, when 145 students were taught by five teachers in four different buildings, tenders were finally called for a new school of five classrooms with laboratory and science room. This became the first high school. W. Dezell and Son of Williams Lake secured the contract for $22,000. Mrs Earley, Quesnel's first teacher, cut the ribbon and opened the new school; with her were John A. Fraser and A. S. Vaughan who had been on the school board for twenty-five years. The ceremony took place on August 31, 1937. By the time the new school was opened, the Parent-Teacher Association was well organized with Mrs. John Freeman as president. Three years later Mrs. Pauline Yahlonitsky became the first school nurse and won great support for the dental clinic inaugurated the following year.

Throughout British Columbia school boards were having difficulties, and a Royal Commission under Dr. Maxwell Cameron was appointed to investigate the financial conditions of provincial schools. The sixteen school boards in the Quesnel district presented a brief to Dr. Cameron that was almost prophetic. Under the new plan of centralized education, Quesnel became the centre for North Cariboo School District Number 28. Moose Heights to, but not including Soda Creek came into this district, as did schools from Baker Lake and Nazko to Wells and Barkerville. This latter area believed it should be a separate school district but because of its decreasing population officials did not agree.

At the end of the war the local school with nearly 200 pupils was again overcrowded. By September 1946 there were 240 pupils and though four rooms were required no space was available for rent. In their usual forthright manner, the people passed a plebiscite to raise $168,500 for a new high school, which was subsequently built in 1950, a dormitory being erected in 1957. In 1949 two of the first Quonset hut schools had been erected at Alexandria and Castle

Rock. An elementary school was built in West Quesnel in 1953, and a junior high in 1957.

Twenty schools constituted the district; the twelve new rural school buildings planned in 1952 had been built of plywood at an approximate cost of $504,000, $282,000 of which was raised by borrowing. Wells had a Superior School. Within Quesnel town limits there were 1,000 students, while 2,300 comprised the school district. The "old log school," Quesnel's second government-built school, was eventually used for teaching in the day time and at night was used as a library and meeting place of the Cariboo Historical Society. That old school building of the old town had also been used for church services at one time, but ultimately the village had real churches.

The Hudson's Bay Company often took priests and preachers to forts, but did not do so readily in New Caledonia. Peter Skene Ogden asked for contributions from his personnel, Catholic and Protestant, to assist the Catholic cause in Washington, but did nothing for the northern district. Father De Smet had recently established a mission near Willamette and in 1842 went to Fort Vancouver to discuss with the Canadian missionaries the best way to extend the mission northward. At this meeting the Rev. Father M. Demers was chosen to open a new mission field in New Caledonia and he thus became the first missionary in the interior of British Columbia. Born at St. Jean-Chrysostome, Quebec, on October 11, 1808, he had studied at the seminary in nearby Quebec City. He was ordained February 7, 1836, and the following year went to Red River and thence to Colville and Fort Vancouver. Peter Skene Ogden was at this last fort for the yearly outfit to New Caledonia and agreed to transport Father Demers to the north. In a letter to the Bishop of Quebec, dated at Fort Alexandria on December 20, 1842 this brave and ardent "Black Robe," as the priests were known, told of his travels by Hudson's Bay Company brigade, and reported on the new mission field.

Obviously New Caledonia and its main river had not received much publicity to that date. Father Demers even mistook the origin of the river's name: "Fort Alexandria is on the 53rd degree of latitude, on the Fraser River, and owes its name, as well as that of the river to Sir Alexander Fraser who discovered it." At this point

Father Demers saw the state of the Indians, the "Porteurs" or "Carriers," and determined to make them the chief object of his concern. He was appalled by their condition and set himself to convert them. The Company offered him room on a barge going north to Fort George and Fort Stuart, but before he left Alexandria he baptized sixty-seven children.

On his return to Alexandria he persuaded the "savages" to build a chapel and so began the first church in Cariboo. Father Demers then went south to Williams Lake where he obtained land for the mission. Returning to Alexandria, he helped finish the chapel, where he held the first holy mass on December 4, 1842. The exact site of the church is difficult to determine, but it was no doubt close to the fort. It was of log and a fair size: "A cross decorated one of the gables and a chimney placed at the other end served to heat the chapel in cold weather." Lacking glass they probably used skins over the windows, as they had done at Williams Lake, but of that place he said, "Annoyingly ill-luck, if some wretchedly famished dogs didn't eat our windows!"

Until the gold rush Roman Catholic missionaries were the only ones to penetrate the district and to bring Christianity to white and native alike, and because it was already in the area the Church of Rome first carried the gospel over the Cariboo Mountains into the roaring gold camps. In 1861 Father Charles Grandidier visited miners and Indians on the river, going as far as Williams Creek. He was followed by Father L. Fouquet who established the mission Father Demers had started at Williams Lake. Father Grandidier had walked into the gold district in 1861, but the church did not formally go into the gold fields until 1865, when Father Gendre celebrated 11 o'clock mass every Sunday at Richfield. Father Gendre left before the winter of 1866, and Father Magoggin arrived the next summer, bought a house at Richfield and prepared it as a place of worship. Two years later Bishop L. J. De Herbomez, D. D. passed ten days at the Cariboo mines and on July 19, 1868 dedicated the hall and bell of St. Patrick's Catholic Church at Richfield, which was occupied that summer by Fathers Jolivet and McGuickin. While the Bishop was at Richfield, he was welcomed by all, both Catholics and Protestants contributing to a fund for him.

The Church of England, too, sent missionaries into the gold fields. During 1861 the Rev. C. Knipe and R. Lunden Brown were on Williams Creek and were followed by James Sheepshanks and Mr. Dundas. They all preached in Antler, Van Winkle and Cottonwood. In 1863 the church on Williams Creek was made permanent. The site was chosen and a contract was let to build a church; it cost $1,200 raised by contributions and seated 120 persons—"a small substantial, well-proportioned building." Sheepshanks took in a library of about 250 books. The mission then fell vacant for two years until the Rev. James Reynard went to lead the Anglicans of Cariboo. He bought an old building in Barkerville for use as a church on Sunday and as a school building during the week. Within two months of his arrival the great fire wiped out his efforts. Services were then held in Reynard's home and later above a workshop. By June 1869 he was canvassing for funds to build a new church; by November men were working on it at the lower end of Barkerville. After many delays because of insufficient funds, St. Saviour's Episcopal Church was opened by the Rev. James Reynard on September 18, 1870. Because it was built on a mining claim, in April 1871 application was made for free title to the land. St. Saviour's still stands almost as the *Cariboo Sentinel* described it during construction:

> The new church (S. Saviour's) now building, promises to be an elegant structure. It is built from designs by the Rev. J. Reynard, which are being ably carried out by Messrs. Bruce & Mann. The style is "Early English," in which architectural effect is attained by due proportion of parts, bold and simple forms, rather than by elaborate ornament. The church will consist of — nave, 30 ft. x 20 ft., and apsidal chancel, 16 ft. x 12 ft. Height of walls, 18 feet; of ceiling, from floor, 23 feet. A schoolroom and vestry complete the building. We congratulate the friends of the Anglican Church on possessing a church so appropriate to their worship. Certainly those who wish to pray, as their fathers prayed, may do so here, in a church which in form, if not in material, will remind them of the village churches of the "fatherland."

Not only were there Roman Catholics and Anglicans on the Creek, but also Methodists, Presbyterians and a Welsh group. The Wesleyan Methodists were represented for four months in 1863 by Rev. Ephraim Evans and Rev. Arthur Browning, but until 1868 by no others. Finally the Rev. Thomas Derrick built a church which was dedicated on June 20, 1869.

By far the most popular missionary was the first and only Presbyterian minister in Cariboo before Confederation, the Rev. D. Duff, and his popularity increased when he remained with his flock for the winter. He stayed for thirteen months, holding morning services for the Church of Scotland at Camerontown, and afternoon services at Richfield. His was "the longest period any clergyman... remained in this inhospitable region...." and even he could not endure permanent residence on the Creek.

In 1866 the large Welsh group led by John Evans built the Cambrian Hall for religious services. After the fire Evans rebuilt on the old site, but by this time the mines were less rich, and the Cambrian Society achieved no great success.

At Quesnellemouth the first church was Roman Catholic, built probably in 1864 by Rev. Father Pierre Fouquet. Father Fouquet's church burned in 1871. Although a Chinese was blamed for the fire, no definite proof was found. Not until 1902 was St. Ann's Church built by Father Thomas of St. Joseph's Mission. From 1871 to 1902 priests making circuit came to Quesnel three times each year to hold mass in the most convenient house. Baptism, marriage and religious instruction had to wait until he came around, although burials were performed by one of the household reading a prayer. After the church was built, services were held once a month by priests from St. Joseph's.

The Protestants were not so well served. Although the Rev. Mr. James Reynard from Barkerville had included Quesnel in his parish of 2,500 people, after 1888 all Protestants used the school building for Sunday worship. No Protestant church was built until 1895 when, under the auspices of a Presbyterian, the Rev. Dr. A. D. McKinnon, a Union Church was built and used by all until 1911 at which time the Anglican Mission was introduced. In the fall of 1911 the Presbyterians erected a new church when the Anglicans purchased the Union Church for use until their new one was completed in 1913. The Guild of St. Mary, the Anglican Women's group, formed that year. This new church burned in 1923, and the congregation again used the old Union Church building until another was consecrated on September 5, 1925. The old Union Church finally became a warehouse on Kinchant Street between Carson and Johnston avenues. In 1911 the Mission of St. John the Divine had sent five priests and two laymen to Quesnel to begin a mission. One of the first preachers was Samuel Pollinger who later, in 1942, became Bishop of Cariboo, but died at Kamloops only eight months after assuming office.

The Presbyterian influence was strong in Quesnel where many of the inhabitants were of Maritime-Scottish descent. On November 19, 1911 St. Andrew's Presbyterian Church opened with the Rev. William Stott as preacher. The following year the Ladies' Guild and the Literary Guild began functioning. In 1925 the question arose about union with the Methodists as the United Church of Canada. Mr. Petrie, then the minister, opposed union and accepted the Kamloops Presbytery, only to arouse considerable opposition when he changed his mind about staying and about church union. He was, however, re-instated, but was replaced by the Reverend Mr. Thomson a year later, when St. Andrew's did join the United Church of Canada.

CHAPTER TEN

Law and Order

When gold was discovered on the Lower Fraser and the excitement rose to a high pitch, the government appointed justices of the peace to perform duties of nearly all departments. The powers of these men were varied and at times extremely intricate. They had power to settle claim disputes; "lay over," or stop, mining for periods when work was not possible because of weather or when supplies were difficult to obtain; order public works to be done; erect buildings; have projects carried out for the public safety; try court cases involving less than $250, and preside as judge on mining cases; "mark out for business purposes or gardens...a plot of ground...." Although not technically "judges," many assumed that role and many became known by that name. They were, therefore, the government of the area and saw that order prevailed. For a case requiring a higher decision, they relied on the Supreme Court.

With the advance of the miners northward, officials were necessary in the new region, and on July 17, 1860 Philip Henry Nind took an oath swearing to "honestly and truly perform the duties of Justice of the Peace for the district of Alexandria in the Colony of British Columbia...." He was the first government official posted to the area. As chief constable, William Pinchbeck went with him. Nind chose Williams Lake as his headquarters because of its location near the junction of the river and the old brigade trails. From there he could travel in all directions, and immediately after his arrival at Williams Lake went to Alexandria and then to Ferguson's Bar, about six miles from the mouth of the Quesnel River.

He went there because of the trouble created by Moses Anderson, the miner who had shot an Indian boy. Nind pacified the native villagers and appointed Isaac Holden a special constable to arrest Anderson, and thus Holden may be considered the first constable in Quesnel.

Nind then had to report on his activities and did so on October 17, 1860:

> Immediately my presence became known on the Bar [Ferguson's Bar] great satisfaction was expressed by the most respectable of the community at the arrival of a Peace Officer amongst them as they had hitherto felt beyond the pale of the law and protection and completely at the mercy of a few drunken desperadoes.

Philip Henry Nind, and those who followed him, organized the civil development of the country. Nind granted mining licences and recorded claims; granted permission to build bridges and to run ferries; made recommendations on petitions, and travelled the country establishing jails and communities, administering justice and writing reports to his superiors. Of all the early officials of this district, Nind was the most imaginative. He was a fluent writer, and his letters, more than those of any other official, sketch a picture of the settlements, transportation and prices in early Cariboo. Because officials' wages were low and travelling allowances were inadequate in an area where prices were high, Nind had trouble keeping his deputies. On December 9, 1861 he applied for leave of absence because of illness.

Before he had gone to Alexandria, Nind had discussed the feasibility of a Gold Escort to ensure safe delivery of treasure to Victoria at a small charge for each ounce of gold carried. This plan was instituted in 1861 with charges from Quesnel Forks at one shilling an ounce. The government equipped a handsomely uniformed, well mounted and adequately armed group of twelve men, with guards from the Royal Engineers. But because the government would not guarantee delivery, the miners would not patronize the escort and continued to carry their own earnings.

In 1863 the plan was revived following a brutal murder and

robbery which had taken place in the summer of 1862 at Quesnel Forks. Thomas Elwyn was in charge of the new escort of fifteen men and Nind was superintendent. Once again the project failed; only the banks used the convenience; miners still preferred to trust their luck. They still had no guarantee of delivery, and rumours of lost receipts and treasury officials releasing supposedly confidential figures to newspapers undermined confidence. When in 1863 the Escort cost the colony $60,000 and grossed only $9,000, the miners joined the rest of the population in decrying the plan.

Nind was granted his leave of absence in 1862 and was replaced by Thomas Elwyn who appointed L. T. Seymour as his Chief Constable. At Quesnel Forks, where a large group of men had congregated, Elwyn rented a building for a temporary office. By that year, the district had become larger and busier; Elwyn recognized the need for several permanent stations rather than merely one at Williams Lake. In July he called for tenders to build at Richfield a house 16 feet by 30 feet, partitioned to make an office and a court room at cost of 295. On writing to the Colonial Secretary about the matter, he said,

> Some government buildings on this creek will always be required: even should it not be made the Head Quarters of a Magistrate, I would suggest that the Creek should never be left without some official.

Along with the request for increased government stations Elwyn advised dividing Cariboo District into two sections with two magistrates. He himself took the eastern part, the mining area with most work, while Peter O'Reilly went to work in the western portion, including the mouth of the Quesnel. That fall of 1862 Elwyn laid-over the mining until spring, left a constable in charge, and proceeded south.

The Gold Commissioner had difficulty in employing men in a land which seemed to be one vast field of gold, especially while wages given by the Colonial government remained extremely low. Many resigned to work the creeks; others panned a little gold in their spare time. Elwyn himself could not resist the temptation to speculate and bought a share in a claim on rich Williams Creek. On his way south that winter he read a copy of the *Colonist* dated October 21, 1862 which criticized officials who owned property in the mining area. He wrote his superiors immediately to refute charges that justice was not being properly weighed, but resigned his appointment saying, "the claim has of late become so valuable that I cannot in justice to myself abandon it...." The resignation was accepted, but the following year, having done poorly in mining, he joined the government Gold Escort.

Peter O'Reilly transferred to Cariboo East and William G. Cox went to Cariboo West. O'Reilly was exceedingly popular with the miners and earned their respect with his democratic ways. In his time a democratically elected Mining Board was constituted to advise the Gold Commissioner on mining affairs, and O'Reilly himself generally took advice on alterations or amendments to rules and regulations, and on working or holding claims. When O'Reilly later went to Wild Horse Creek in the Kootenay, Cox handled both sections of Cariboo until H. M. Ball became Magistrate at Quesnel. When Cox became Acting Colonial Secretary from October 1865 until November 1866 W. R. Spalding relieved him of his duties at the mines until he returned.

After the union of the colonies of British Columbia and Vancouver Island, the Governor was empowered to appoint stipendiary magistrates or justices of the peace to be county court judges. Spalding went to Nanaimo-Comox and Henry M. Ball became County Court Judge of Cariboo in September 1867.

Because of troubles on Grouse Creek in 1867, Chartres Brew himself went to Cariboo. He had come to the colony from the Irish Constabulary to organize the police in 1858 and had become Chief Gold Commissioner and Superintendent of Magistrates at New Westminster. Ball took charge of the New Westminster district in the meantime, and the whole of Cariboo north of Soda Creek fell within Brew's jurisdiction. He died on Williams Creek on May 31, 1870 and was buried in the local cemetery. On Brew's death, Ball once more administered Cariboo. As magistrate he handed down lesser judgements, as Gold Commissioner he judged mining cases, and as County Court Judge sat on civil cases. He was there until 1881 when all lay judges were retired and only professional men retained.

Three years later, in 1884, Eli Harrison became Stipendiary Magistrate and County Court Judge for Cariboo. He was replaced by Clement Francis Cornwall of Ashcroft who had resigned a

Senatorship to become Lieutenant-Governor of British Columbia. Cornwall held the post until 1907 when Frederick Calder became County Court Judge. He did not retire until 1939 and was succeeded by J. O. Wilson of Prince George. Henry Castillou, a native son of Cariboo, then became the incumbent.

While Ball was Magistrate and Gold Commissioner for Cariboo, John Bowron, the postmaster at Barkerville, became constable at Richfield, and F. Trevor became constable at Quesnel. Three years later, in 1875, Bowron became Government Agent and though he performed the duties of Gold Commissioner, he only received the title officially in 1881. John Bowron had been a leading citizen of Barkerville since he arrived with the Overlanders of 1862, and he remained there until he retired and then died in 1906. His place was taken by J. McKen who stayed but three months before being replaced by G. J. Walker. In Quesnel there was no government official except Provincial Police Constable D. H. Anderson, who remained until 1912 when F. Islip took over the duties. In 1909 G. E. Stephenson became Deputy Mining Recorder at Quesnel, having been removed from a redundant agency at the Forks, but this new agency lasted only one year.

Barkerville was becoming less and less important, and the government offices were to be moved to a greater centre of population. As a result of the combined efforts of the Board of Trade and John A. Fraser, M.L.A., Quesnel was chosen instead of Prince George. In May 1914 the new Quesnel Court House opened with G. Milbourn as Government Agent, H. T. Kraemer as clerk and Deputy Mining Recorder, Percy Foot, C. F. Boyd, H. P. Vaughn and L. C. Maclure as clerks. This move made Quesnel the centre of the area and Barkerville became a sub-agency.

While Cariboo was a centre of world attention, newspapers carried commentaries on conditions in the area. On August 17, 1863 the *Colonist* reported the absence of crime:

> Everything is very quiet and orderly on the Creek owing in great measure to Mr. O'Reilly's efficiency and the wholesome presence of Judge Begbie who seems to be a terror to evil doers and a sworn enemy to the use of the knife and revolver. Crime in Cariboo has been vigorously checked in its infancy by a firm hand, and seems to have brought some soil more congenial to its growth. The most prej-

udiced of foreigners on the Creek allow that a security of life and property exists which twelve months ago it would have appeared as useless to expect.

Although the local constables, magistrates and county court judges were active in the area, criminal cases were tried before Judge Matthew Baillie Begbie. He had come to North America at the same time as Chartres Brew and, as the choice of Sir Edward Bulwer Lytton, became Judge of the Crown Colony of British Columbia. Begbie supervised the administration of justice in the colony and this he did adequately with the assistance of gold commissioners and magistrates who were supported by Brew's police force.

Begbie rode through the country holding court as formally as possible under the circumstances, and attending to government business. Fearless and just, with a rough and ready reasoning that at times defied precedent while at the same time teaching respect for the law, he advocated the "cat o' nine tails." He firmly believed, over Brew's objections, that "if a man insists on behaving like a brute, after fair warning, and won't quit the Colony; treat him like a brute and flog him."

His Honour's fame spread yearly as he made both friends and enemies while dispensing his unconventional justice. Peter O'Reilly, with Begbie until a few moments before he died in 1894, was one of his greatest friends; others, such as Lt. Palmer, had little use for him. When Elwyn resigned his post as Magistrate at Alexandria he had also received a warning from his superiors about officials having mining interests. Judge Begbie, nevertheless, became involved in a scandal when his ownership of twenty acres at Cottonwood was revealed and the information used to detract from his stature as a judge. Others believed that the terrain more than the influence of Begbie prevented crime in the northern area of the colony, and said that because renegades could not possibly escape from the territory they did not enter. In any case, order prevailed on the creeks, and because Begbie's judgements were severe he must have been a contributing force despite criticism. The epithet "the hanging Judge" came not from the fact that he condemned many to death, for he did not, but rather from the way he might speak of criminals or the way in which he might admonish a jury. At one time when the jury brought in a verdict of manslaughter at a trial where a gunman might have been found guilty of deliberate murder, the Judge is reputed to have turned his wrath on the group, saying,

> Had the jury performed their duty I might now have the painful satisfaction of condemning you to death, and you, gentlemen of the jury, you are a pack of Dalles horse thieves, and permit me to say, it would give me great pleasure to see you hanged, each and every one of you, for declaring a murderer guilty of only manslaughter.

The noted Judge held court from his horse, in stables, in the open or in properly established court houses across the length and breadth of his territory, the largest in the British Empire. He held court in Richfield, where he had a private residence, sentencing criminals, hearing appeals and dispensing justice. Many times, too, he heard cases in Quesnel, the most famous being the trials of the Indians sentenced for the massacre of the Waddington surveyors. The jail at Quesnel had been erected in 1863, but was seldom used before these trials and little used after them. In 1866 the townspeople appealed to the Judge for repairs to the jail because the green timbers used in constructing the doors had shrunk "so that the bolts of the locks will not catch." The jail was repaired.

No Court of Assize was held in Quesnel for over forty years until Judge Robertson sat on a hearing in 1916, and then not again until 1934 with Chief Justice Morrison on the bench.

Barkerville Quesnel & the Cariboo Gold Rush

Quesnel & District Museum & Archives
In the Barkerville Cemetery

New Advertisements.

STEAM TO CARIBOO !

The British Columbia

GENERAL TRANSPORTATION COMPANY

Will place Four of THOMSON'S PATENT ROAD STEAM-ERS on the route between Yale and Barkerville in the First Week in April, and will be prepared to enter into Contracts for the conveyance of Freight from Yale to Soda Creek in EIGHT DAYS. Through Contracts will be made as soon as the condition of the road above Quesnelmouth permits.

Rates of Passage will be advertised in due time.

BARNARD & BEEDY,   anagers.

OFFICE—Yates Street, next door to Wells, Fargo & Co.'s

Advertisement from *Daily British Colonist*

June 20th, 1866.   Barkerville. 14

PREVENTION IS BETTER THAN CURE

Moses' Hair Invigorator.

TO PREVENT BALDNESS, restore hair that has fallen off or become thin, and to cure effectually Scurf or Dandruff. It will also relieve the Headache, and give the hair a darker and glossy color, and the free use of it will keep both the skin and hair in a healthy state. Ladies will find the Invigorator a great addition to toilet, both in consideration of the delicate and agreeable perfume, and the great facility it affords in dressing the hair, which, when moist with it, can be dressed in any required form, so as to preserve its place, whether plain or in curls. When used on children's heads, it lays the foundation for a good head of hair.

Prepared only by   W. D. MOSES,
Barkerville, Williams Creek.

Advertisement from *Cariboo Sentinel*

TO THE

Electors of Cariboo

WE, the undersigned electors of Cariboo, residing in Barkerville, the home of Dr. Watt for the past eight years, have no hesitation in stating that we place no confidence in him as a politician. His utterances here have always been in condemnation of the Conservative Government, which he now professes to support.

We, moreover, deprecate his present move in opposing Mr. Barnard after giving him every assurance that it was unnecessary to continue his canvass as he (Watt) did not intend to be a candidate.

ED OGDEN,	N WILCOX,
W. WILLEY,	P HOWLEY,
W. C. PRICE,	ALEX LOCK,
ROBT HEATH,	JHO BOWKEN,
ALEX COUTTS,	P McDERMOTT,
GOMER JOHNS,	JAS STEWART,
GEO FERGUSON,	ARNOLD WILSON,
MAT PINKERTON,	ANDREW KELLEY,
WM HODGKINSON,	THEO SAYARGENT
WALTER HUSKINSON,	

Election poster

Theatre Royal, Barkerville.

LAFONT
AND
WARD'S
TROUPE

WILL APPEAR ON

Sunday Evening, July 26th,

PROGRAMME

CHINA ACT.

MASQUERADE BALL,

CARD OF THANKS

Thanking all those electors in the Cariboo Riding who voted for me in the recent election, and also those who said they were going to, but who didn't.

C. T. DOCHERTY

NOTICE

Playbill

Cariboo Observer

Card of Thanks--Docherty

Quesnel & District Museum & Archives/Kennett Collection
Freight on Cariboo Wagon Road, ca.1910

Quesnel & District Museum & Archives
B.C. Express Stage at 153 Mile

Quesnel & District Museum & Archives -Windt Collection
B.C. Express Co. at Quesnel ca. 1900

Quesnel & District Museum & Archives
Unloading First Air Mail at Quesnel – August 4, 1938

Quesnel & District Museum & Archives -Windt Collection
Freight Teams at Ashcroft

Mrs. J.M. Yorston
Andrew Olson and John Yorston demonstrating one-wheeled barrow

Quesnel & District Museum & Archives
Dog Pack Team at Hudson's Bay Co. – Quesnel, 1910

Quesnel Cariboo Observer
Cataline's Pack Train at Quesnel, ca. 1900

Quesnel & District Museum & Archives -Kennett Collection
90 HP Oldsmobile – Beaver Pass House, ca. 1910-1914

Quesnel & District Museum & Archives -City 0f Quesnel/Bohanon Collection
Cattle for Slaughter in Barkerville

Quesnel & District Museum & Archives -Windt Collection
Dredge at Antler Creek near Barkerville, 1925

Quesnel & District Museum & Archives -Windt Collection
Barkerville – St. Saviour's Church on right

Quesnel & District Museum & Archives -Carson Collection
Main Street Barkerville, 1929

Quesnel & District Museum & Archives -Carson Collection
Bill Livingstone delivering mail – Barkerville ca. 1920

Quesnel & District Museum & Archives -Carson Collection
Archie Boyd, Main Street Barkerville, ca. 1920s

Quesnel & District Museum & Archives -Carson Collection
C.S. Wing on right – Tailings Pile near Barkerville, Nov. 4, 1913

Quesnel & District Museum & Archives - Windt Collection
**Henry & Alex Windt – Hydraulic Placer Mining,
Canadian Creek near Barkerville, 1899**

Quesnel & District Museum & Archives
Quesnel, ca.1890

Quesnel & District Museum & Archives
Quesnel Hockey Team leaving for Barkerville c.1913

Quesnel & District Museum & Archives
Quesnel Hockey Team vs. Barkerville c.1918

Quesnel & District Museum & Archives
Front Street ca. 1880s

Quesnel & District Museum & Archives - Quesnel Historical Society
Front Street, Quesnel c.1897

Quesnel & District Museum & Archives - Quesnel Historical Society
China Town, Quesnel c. 1900

Quesnel & District Museum & Archives -Quesnel Historical Society
Front Street, Quesnel c.1911

Quesnel & District Museum & Archives - Carson Collection
WWI Recruits heading out on B.X – June 1, 1915

Quesnel & District Museum & Archives - Windt Collection
Chilcotin and B.X. - Quesnel

The B.X. – the only sternwheeler with a covered wheel

B.X., B.C. Express and Chilcotin dry docked at Quesnel c.1915

Quesnel & District Museum & Archives
The Charlotte wrecked on rocks in Fort George Canyon

Quesnel & District Museum & Archives - Windt Collection
Reid Sawmill, Quesnel, c. 1911

Quesnel & District Museum & Archives - Windt Collection
Women's Foot Race, Quesnel, July 1, 1910

Quesnel & District Museum & Archives - Carson Collection
Ladies Hockey Match, Quesnel, c. 1915

The Bachelors of the 150-Mile House and vicinity request the pleasure of the company of *Mr. Mrs. Bohaun* at the 150-Mile House, on the evening of February 2nd, 1898, at 8 p.m. The lady patronesses of the evening will be Mrs. Herald and Mrs. Adams. Dancing

R. Borland,
President.

A. C. Knight,
Secretary.

R.S.V.P.

Quesnel & District Museum & Archives -City of Quesnel Collection
Dance Invitation , 1898

Quesnel & District Museum & Archives -Windt Collection
Dance at the Rex Theatre

CHAPTER ELEVEN

Government

The Colonial and Provincial governments were responsible for the development of the Quesnel townsite. In very early days, through the gold rush period and the minor excitements that followed, the government looked after the area well, but after 1895 when the settlement lost its importance the authorities ignored the streets, roads and general condition of the town. In 1910 local merchants became exasperated with this lack of interest shown a settlement which had stores, hotels, warehouses, shipping offices and other business. As the area regained its former importance with railway construction to the north, it became apparent that a Board of Trade was necessary to press the claims of the town and district for many needed public facilities and to manage local affairs.

In March 1910 a formation meeting was called with J. Holt as Chairman and A. W. Healy as secretary, a meeting which decided that an election of officers be held the following month. The Board of Trade had been formally organized. In April A. W. Cameron, manager of the Northern Crown Bank, was elected president, and S. L. Hilborn, a farmer, vice-president, with J. L. Hill, a fisheries overseer, as secretary. An Executive committee elected to represent both town and district included A. W. Healy, store manager, E. L. Kepner, hotel owner, and three farmers, J. Holt, W. T. Ewing and R. M. Yorston. The district covered by this new organization included the settlements at Barkerville, 150 Mile House and Soda Creek.

Almost immediately the group began its campaign to make life more pleasant for the people of the district, especially for those of the larger concentrations of population. It hoped to attract the attention of the rest of the province by publicizing Cariboo, as well as to handle civic development through organized appeals to the local populations and to government officials. In the summer of 1910 the government held a sale of lots at the instigation of the Board, which also brought lecturers into town to interest people in a fur breeding industry.

In general the Board of Trade backed community enterprises and tried to curb the slovenliness into which the town was slipping after having been ignored so long. For example, the old cemetery, with its first headboard dated 1865, had become too small; some of the graves had been used twice; the gate-hooks had been stolen, and cattle were allowed to wander undisturbed through the weeds. The Board first demanded a new site in 1912, and over the years it appointed various committees to investigate possibilities on Two Mile Flat and on Red Bluff Hill, but finally arranged with the government in 1916 to use town Block 63.

Animals wandered the streets, ate the grass which the Board of Trade had planted along the river bank, and broke garden fences. Such a general nuisance forced the Board to attempt a pound law, but the plan failed. Because the area was not legally organized, the pound keeper, through his attempts to interfere with people's stock, was taken to court. John A. Fraser, as M.L.A., then had the Pound Districts Act altered, but Quesnel's pound came to nothing after incorporation, despite items in the *Cariboo Observer* which forgot that the "authorities" it referred to had no authority: "There are several bulls of varying ages, roaming at large through the town, contrary to law. It is up to the authorities to take action in this matter before a regrettable accident occurs."

The dumping of garbage on the flat south of town was eventually prohibited. A new government road to Dragon Lake was built at the instigation of the Board, and at its suggestion the telegraph office and post office were separated. When it protested volubly against removal of all government offices from Barkerville to Prince George rather than to Quesnel, the junction town obtained its government buildings. To soothe Prince George, the Board then began immediate demands for road and telegraph connections between the two towns. The former came in 1924, the latter in 1926. When the road was assured the Board allocated a tourist campsite.

The rough and muddy streets of the town were supervised by the district road superintendent, and several times each year the Board of Trade managed to have them graded and topped with good gravel from Red Bluff Hill. In 1911 the sidewalks were in a state of collapse. Property owners had built wooden walks in front of their own property, but accidents were occurring regularly when the passersby tripped on rotten boards. Added to the accident hazard was the inconvenience of having no complete sidewalk all of one level. Demands were therefore made that the government erect a level sidewalk. By 1913 new plank walks were constructed on Front Street and on Carson Avenue as far as Yan War's corner and, in 1914, along Barlow to the Court House and along Carson to the churches. While running the town, however, the Board did fail to have a bridge span the Fraser although it sent a yearly plea to the government.

Generally, the Quesnel Board of Trade had a remarkable record in advancing the community, but by 1927 it needed far more money to carry out its activities. The Board had been kept operating through subscriptions and had no way of raising funds, but knowing that as an incorporated municipality the village would share profits of the Government Liquor Vendor, which had been opened in 1921 by J. J. Donnelly, and share in motor vehicle licences and in pari-mutuel betting, and knowing that an incorporated area plans its own future, the Board of Trade petitioned the government for incorporation. Although the Board has been of less civic importance since incorporation, it has been a force behind the Commissioners of the Village, and in most cases the chairman of the Village Commissioners was a member of the Board, if not its president. Over successive years the Board worked for regulated store closing hours, town planning, cement sidewalks in 1938, street surfacing by the Public Works Department, and industrial zoning. These projects were all proposed by the Commissioners, but in many cases were first advanced by the Board of Trade.

The British Columbia *Gazette* of March 29, 1928 carried the notice of the incorporation of North Quesnel and Quesnel, but not the district across the Fraser River, West Quesnel: "The said [newly created] municipality shall be called and known by the name and style of "The Corporation of the Village of Quesnel." The *Gazette* showed Charles H. Allison, druggist, Albert J. Elliott, theatre owner, and John G. Hutchcroft, publisher, appointed as Board of Commissioners of the municipality until an election should be held. A. S. Vaughan was appointed Clerk. With Miss Maud Carson as Returning Officer and Vaughan her Deputy, four candidates for three seats stood in Quesnel's first civic election on May 26, 1928. Hutchcroft declined to run; F. W. Pinchbeck polled 39 votes; A. J. Elliott, 33; C. H. Allison, 32; T. Marion, 20. E. J. Avison became Village Solicitor.

As early as 1929 the new village was planning the new municipal hall which was erected the following year, had passed early closing laws for businesses—6:30 daily except Saturday with a half-day holiday Thursday—had arranged for the installation of light and water, and had a surplus amounting to over $1,200. Since that time schools have been built, cement sidewalks laid out, industrial zoning laws passed, town planning considered, lanes surveyed, and streets surfaced. By and large, the municipality has been better managed in a more progressive manner than most in the province. The greatest achievement in earliest times was the arranging for light and water. With incorporation came renewed hope for electric lights to eliminate the necessity of lamps and candles, and for an adequate water supply for sewage and fire protection.

Quesnel had a series of proposals for lighting the town. In 1910 W. McMullen, H. L. Stoddard and Ross Mackenzie decided to supply the settlement with electricity. When they failed the *Cariboo Observer* increased its advertisements for the latest in gas lamps. In 1920 the Quesnel Timber and Trading Company talked of furnishing lights, but offered nothing definite. The first positive plan came in 1921 when the Pacific Great Eastern Railway, which was then completed to Quesnel, proposed to install a plant capable of handling the light and water needs of the town and which would become private or public property after ten years. The plant was to be steam driven and to have a water pump at the end of Bowron Avenue, and the standpipe was to be located on the high bench north of Reginald Boothe's property. At that time no organization was authorized to make agreements and the Pacific Great Eastern therefore built for itself only. The Quesnel Telephone Company then talked of installing a plant, but its plan also faded. Local residents were aware of the well-lighted and convenient railway yards and fully realized the advantage of electricity.

Certain businesses installed their own plants. In 1923 J. C. Cowan opened his new hardware store and installed a plant; in 1927 the owners of the Cariboo Hotel wired their property for electricity. By the time of incorporation J. W. Pearson was supplying a number of businesses and residences with light, but the old street lighting system continued: on dark nights in 1912, Hutchcroft and the Reid Estate had placed lanterns on the streets.

In January 1929 the Village Commissioners introduced a street lighting plant that was totally inadequate, and because of its inadequacy they met with O. S. Metz and R. Ballantyne to discuss the possibility of water and light for Quesnel. Metz and Ballantyne planned to erect a lighting plant on Baker Creek, a plant run with a water wheel and with an auxiliary in town. The man behind the plan was David Grierson.

Quesnel was to have twelve street lamps of 100 watts each. The town was to pay $1,200 a year plus $125 a year bonus for the decrease in insurance premium. The company to be formed was to have a twenty-five-year franchise, tax free for ten years. Water was to cost householders $5 a year, and light $3 a month. The Commissioners felt that this price was beyond reason and refused the offer. They demanded free fire and street washing water along with twenty street lamps of 100 watts and a flat rate of $50 a month. Any company being formed would be required to assume the Commissioners' street lighting venture. The service would be better on this plan and the costs would be $750 a year less.

David Grierson accepted these demands, obtained the rights on June 18, 1929, and operated as the Quesnel Light, Heat, Power and Water Company until he sold to the Quesnel Light and Water Company Limited on July 25. This company had a capital of $40,000 and 400 shares of which 100 shares were retained by Grierson. Almost immediately work was commenced to bring three lines of 2,300 volts each from a Baker Creek lease, three and a half miles from the Fraser on Pacific Great Eastern land. By mid-July 1930 the town was lighted electrically. Light was supplied to homes until 1 a.m. at the regular monthly price; after that time at $2 an hour. Twelve hours were given free to the town. Five years later twenty-four hour service was instituted.

In 1935 the depression-ridden Quesnel Light and Water Company mortgaged its assets to the Montreal Trust Company and issued debentures of $30,000 to Pacific Power and Water Company Limited. Two years later, on May 16, 1937, the generator overheated and burned the hydro-electric plant to the ground. The fire began at 1:30 a.m. on a Sunday, but within two hours the standby plant was in use.

A new site on Baker Creek, a new turbine from Ontario, and a plant opened in September. The following year, 1938, the Canada Permanent Trust Company took over from the Montreal Trust Company as nominee of the Pacific Power and Water Company Limited. With the advent of the British Columbia Power Commission in the area, that huge enterprise expropriated the Pacific Power and Water Company properties on July 31, 1945 in order to serve 289 customers. In October 1957 a new station generating 12,830 horsepower officially opened to serve 2,010 consumers.

The formation of the lighting company also meant the coming of running water for Quesnel. The village had always obtained water from the two rivers, or from wells; the supply was good, but inconvenient. When Metz and Ballantyne met the Commissioners in January 1929 they all agreed that the proposed company was to supply five-inch, iron-pipe water mains on Reid and McLean Street. These mains were to be tapped for private use, and a reservoir with pumps was to be built to overcome breakdowns. These pumps, capable of producing one hundred pounds of pressure, were to be used in case of fire. Water from both rivers was analyzed and Quesnel River was found better for domestic use than was Fraser River water.

Work began when the Quesnel Light and Water Company Limited took over from David Grierson. In September a water notice in the *Cariboo Observer* stated that water would be taken 600 yards from the mouth of the Quesnel River, 500 feet northeast of the bridge. Water mains were laid on streets and avenues north of the railroad tracks on Davie Street, north along Kinchant Street to St. Laurent Avenue, along Reid Street to a water tank on the raised ground north of Bowron Avenue overlooking Reid Street. A filter was attached at the intake, and a powerful light on the tank to illuminate the water height indicator. The town paid half the costs of six hydrants and also paid for their installation. These were located at the intersections of Carson and Davie, and Barlow and Kinchant, while on Reid hydrants were located at McNaughton, Shepherd, Barlow and Carson avenues. When at last water flowed in the pipes, the *Cariboo Observer* of December 18, 1929 reported the event:

> When the water was turned into the town mains last week a number of leaks developed, and the company has been busy ever since making repairs. Most of the leaks developed where the main has been tapped to permit future extensions, the pressure forcing the plugs. It also developed, as soon as water was forced into the pressure tank that the foundation on one side had settled six inches, and the contractors rectified this during the week.

Except for winter freeze-ups and complaints about the taste of the water, the system worked well for some years. The British Columbia Power Commission took over the light and power system, but not the water system. The Quesnel Light and Water Company would make no improvements although the system was becoming dilapidated and dangerous. At the end of the war, an increased population found the small water system inadequate. The town's growth had been phenomenal—building costs were over a half-million dollars a year—but the water system with its low pressure was seen as a factor retarding future expansion. One hundred and thirty more buildings required water than received it.

The Village Commissioners planned to purchase the water system, renew it and install proper sewage, and the necessary by-law, voted on November 14, 1947, indicated that people were tired of wells and of hauling water from the river. They approved spending $20,000 for the system and $80,000 for repairs, mostly for 8½ miles of new pipe. The town paid the bill with debentures certified in June 1948. From a well on the Quesnel River banks two pumps raised water into a 100,000 gallon [U.S. gallon] water tank, which burned in 1956 and had to be replaced. The new water system bringing water from wells near Baker Creek was constructed in 1957, when water mains were also laid in West Quesnel. In 1954 sewers were constructed in the main business area.

Better water supply meant better fire protection. In 1863 the settlement at the mouth of the Quesnel had its first serious fire when the brush along the river burned. In Quesnel, as in all small but busy communities, the fire hazard was always recognized but always ignored. Hotel and restaurants had buckets to dip into the nearby river when a fire occurred, but there was no organized brigade. Quesnel learned little from the Barkerville fire of 1868. That conflagration was too far removed, and although Quesnel people observed the leather buckets of the Williams Creek Volunteer Fire Brigade, they did nothing until their own settlement was touched six years later.

At 2 a.m. December 19, 1874 in a Chinese gambling house in the upper part of the town, an habitual opium smoker went to sleep and left his pipe burning. The place caught fire. Ah Yat burned to death, and the entire block, consisting of Elmore's Store, Johnson's Colonial Restaurant, and the gambling house, disappeared at a cost of over $3,000. Elmore saved his stock but did not rebuild; neither did the Chinese nor Johnson, both of whom lost everything.

This fire frightened the local merchants who immediately contributed money to purchase buckets and an iron triangle to be used as a warning bell. No damage by fire followed and any plan was soon forgotten. The buckets were used for other purposes and the triangle disappeared from its position on the river bank. Fire did destroy an occasional building, but the town was so scattered that no extensive damage was done.

In December 1910 the new Board of Trade appointed C. H. Allison to organize a fire-fighting committee. The Quesnel Volunteer Fire Department was created with R. R. Carver as Chief of a bucket brigade of twenty-five. From somewhere the old triangle fire-alarm reappeared, and someone discovered that the old fire prevention group had a bank balance of $130, untouched since 1896. The usual way of raising money in Quesnel was by a Grand Ball, and one was held in January 1911 for this purpose. With the funds the group bought a 400-pound bell which they placed on a tower made of peeled pine poles located on the town lot at the corner of Carson Avenue and McLean Street.

As usual with so many volunteer organizations, the fire department began with many members, but was soon almost forgotten. Probably it would have been forgotten altogether had not Allison realized that the great danger from fire came in the winter. Homes were heated by stoves, and water for extinguishing flames was difficult to carry at that time. Each winter his wardens checked chimneys and made appropriate recommendations in order to reduce the danger.

Early in the morning of January 16, 1916, however, the most destructive fire in Quesnel's history razed eleven buildings in the business section in five hours at a cost of $250,000. The flames started in the Strand Theatre which adjoined and was part of the New Cariboo Hotel. J. Allen, whose room was immediately above the theatre, sounded the alarm, and John Strand, owner of the hotel, aroused his guests. All escaped, but with nothing more than the clothes they wore.

The flames spread north and south. To the north the fire totally destroyed the building used by Strand as a meat market and by Collins and Foot as a haberdashery, although except for the fixtures the clothing store had been vacated a few days earlier. At this northerly limit, a water brigade of forty or fifty Chinese, with the help of a few others, stopped the fire. To the south of the New Cariboo, flames seized the north annex of the Occidental Hotel, caught the main building, jumped to the south annex, and to the John A. Fraser and Company store. Someone then used gun powder to blast the Bank of British North America building in hopes of stopping the fire. The attempt was in vain and the flames kindled Fraser's Number One Warehouse and then the $20,000 stock of the Cowan Supply Company which was located in the old Reid Estate buildings. A group of men tore down the Fraser Company building while a bucket brigade carried snow to extinguish the flames.

Frantic owners tried to save the contents of their buildings. The New Cariboo saved nothing except liquor stored at a distance from the point of outbreak of fire. Some bedding and furniture was salvaged from the Occidental, as was much of the stock of John A. Fraser and the Cowan Company. Lamb's Barber Shop, Vaughan Realty, and the bank were totally destroyed. Fraser, carrying only $12,000 insurance, lost over $20,000 in stock and buildings. E. L. Kepner's Occidental Hotel was valued at $90,000 but was covered by only $15,000 insurance; Kepner's six buildings on Carson Avenue were damaged though not totally destroyed.

Losses were great and morale was low, but some businesses reopened. Cowan moved to temporary quarters in an old billiard hall opposite the boat landing. The Bank of British North America rented the old Express Office in which G. Goudie had operated a library and the express agency in 1866. Fraser used a small warehouse on McLean Street; Strand reopened his meat market in the old Broughton House, also on McLean; W. Lamb, the barber, established north of Marion's store in the next block. The *Cariboo Observer* commented on the great loss:

> For years this town has enjoyed immunity from serious fire which was wonderful, when we consider the natural disadvantages the people have to contend with. Our fire fighting appliances were utterly inadequate to cope with the situation, and it was also apparent in the early stage of the fire that leadership in the fight was lacking ....Perhaps our immunity in the past has made us more or less careless. If so, we have received a lesson—costly, but necessary if we are to avoid similar experiences in the future.

By March the fire brigade was revitalized, with D. R. McLean, J. F. Brady and H. V. Harris as wardens. A suggested underground tank holding 30,000 gallons was considered too costly, but new ladders and buckets were purchased and stored in the Public Works barn for use in case of fire. In 1924 the bell was moved from its original location to the storehouse near the other equipment. But fund-raising was difficult immediately after the fire; people were contributing to war work and charities; then the post-war depression restricted donations, and as a consequence, although partly ready for fire, the town was not totally prepared for the next one.

On June 25, 1925 a fire which broke out in the sleeping quarters of the Good Eats Cafe destroyed most of Quesnel's extensive Chinatown, the government Liquor Store and Reginald Boothe's grocery. The fire spread northward to the Liquor Vendor and south to S. N. Williams and Company on the corner. Boothe's, beside the vendor, was next, followed by the row of Chinese businesses on the north side of Barlow Avenue, between Front and Reid streets. To prevent flames from jumping Barlow Avenue, the forestry pump and hose were brought into play. J. Simister and J. Ericson, two men with rooms in the Good Eats, lost their lives, and it was presumed that the fire started in their rooms when a lamp overturned. C. Davie lost his jewelry store, C. C. Tom his repair shop, Won Kee his laundry, Choo his harness and shoe repair, and Get-a-Som-Sing his buildings. In addition, the Nugget Cafe was lost, as were two unoccupied cabins.

Two fires in less than ten years were all the small town could bear, but without funds and without a water supply little more in the way of fire protection could be procured. Primitive methods of lighting and the lack of water made insurance rates high and policies almost prohibitive. In 1927 the Board of Trade demanded a water survey; the chief reason businessmen appealed for incorporation was for the acquisition of a water system.

Long before water entered the water mains in December 1929, the Village Commissioners had ordered fire hose, and the summer following they purchased a hose-wagon which they stored in the old Seymour Hall from which the Quesnel Fire Department held weekly practices. Two crews were organized, one to fight small fires in the north end of town and one for the south end; in the event of a large fire, both worked. Before water mains were laid, attempts to use a chemical fire-fighting truck had been disappointing and during the depression the village could afford no proper facilities. In 1940, with returning prosperity, the village obtained a truck and 1,300 feet of hose to which another 1,000 feet could be attached if necessary. In 1946 the community bought a real fire truck when the Royal Canadian Air Force sold its Jericho station equipment. The following year the fire department reorganized into one central fire-fighting unit. When the new municipal hall opened in January 1958, two fire trucks were housed in the adjoining fire hall and were operated by the volunteer fire brigade.

Quesnel's fire-fighting equipment became the key to further town expansion. Over the years, especially since 1929 when the long-awaited bridge across the Fraser became a reality, the community on the west shore had been growing rapidly. Its growth was almost too rapid. This district was not incorporated and, although having its own fire protection society, used Quesnel facilities. A scheme was advanced in 1950 whereby West Quesnel would share the cost of a second fire truck for Quesnel if it were available on the west shore in case of fire. West shore property owners opposed the scheme as being too costly. In 1951 some people in West Quesnel wanted to incorporate with Quesnel, and the West Quesnel Fire Association called a meeting in the school for discussion. Leaders of the move saw two definite advantages: they would have fire protection and would share in the greater grant to Quesnel from the Social Security and Municipal Aid Tax. A Quesnel meeting rejected the proposal, countering that the town could not afford a second fire truck.

Again and again the idea of amalgamating the two communities arose. In the spring of 1955 most opposition had died and a plebiscite was held in July. In December West Quesnel became part of Quesnel and the old town increased its population by over 2,000, and its acreage by nearly 800.

The increased size of the community at the river junction called for greater municipal facilities and plans for a new municipal hall. Before long, however, because of the Provincial government's new municipal act, Quesnel began talking of changing its status. In September 1957, Quesnel voted to forsake the rating of village and on January 1, 1958 became one of the first two villages in British Columbia (Mission City was the other) to assume the stature of town. The new Municipal Hall in the new Town of Quesnel opened on January 15, 1958.

Until 1871 British Columbia did not have Responsible Government, but from 1858, with the arrival of so many gold hunters from Canada and the Maritimes where Responsible Government had existed for some years, a definite movement grew, and its goal was a government more responsible to the people. Prior to 1871 the colony was governed by a Legislative Council composed of appointed members: councillors, district magistrates, and five members who were appointed after having been selected by popular poll. The Governor could refuse appointment of selected members, but did not. The members selected for Cariboo were invariably men with mining interests who pledged themselves to promote the removal of road tolls and to improve the mail service. The magistrates of the area were summoned to the Council and had no choice but to go.

The first council on the mainland met in January 1864. Magistrate Peter O'Reilly, James Orr from Cariboo East, and Walter S. Black from Cariboo West represented the mining area. Orr had come to the colony from England early in the decade and had done considerable mining although he was better known as a surveyor. Black, from Australia, was the resident physician at the Cariboo Hospital, as well as chairman of the Mining Board on Williams

Creek; he left the area in 1865 and was killed in an accident near New Westminster in 1871.

For the session of 1864–65 Walter Moberly represented Cariboo West and George A. Walkem Cariboo East. Moberly had gone to Cariboo to supervise the construction of the road from Quesnel to Richfield, and though he was popularly selected, his appointment was widely criticized because the government appeared to be installing one of its own men as one of the five popular members. He was not re-appointed. George Anthony Walkem who replaced Moberly became Premier of the province after Confederation. The district next selected Robert T. Smith who had evinced an interest in Cariboo as early as 1861 when he bid on the mail contract at $500 a month and later built the road from Alexandria to Quesnel.

In 1868 Smith attended the Yale Convention which was called to decided whether or not British Columbia should join the Canadian Confederation. In 1867, after union of the two colonies on the west coast, constituencies were enlarged and Cariboo had only one appointee to the Council in addition to the magistrates. Walkem was the appointee until he became a Justice of the Peace in 1868. During the sessions of 1868–69 and 1870, Robert W. W. Carrall represented Cariboo.

In 1871, British Columbia became a province of the Dominion of Canada and Responsible Government became a reality. To the first Legislative Assembly following Confederation, Cariboo sent three members: G. A. Walkem, Joseph Hunter and Cornelius Booth.

Walkem represented the district from 1871 until 1882. Born in 1834 in Armagh, Northern Ireland, he travelled to Canada in 1858. and in 1862 came to British Columbia where two years later he was admitted to the bar. He was appointed a member of the Legislative Council and was elected to the first legislature. In January 1872 Walkem became Chief Commissioner of Lands and Works, a position he held until December when he became Attorney General. Two years later, on the resignation of Amor de Cosmos, Walkem became Premier, but resigned this position after two years to become leader of the opposition. Elected again in 1878 he became Attorney General once more, Chief Commissioner of Land and Works, and president of the Executive Council. People later felt that Walkem did little for his Cariboo constituency; he had made his home in

Victoria until he died in 1908. Although party labels were not attached until 1903 in British Columbia, Walkem considered himself a Conservative. The second member, Joseph Hunter, a civil engineer, had come from Aberdeen, Scotland, in 1864. After this one term representing Cariboo, he moved to Comox and was twice elected there. Returning to Cariboo to dam the river above Quesnel Forks, in 1900 he again represented Cariboo in the legislature. Until he died in 1935, he too considered himself a Conservative. The third member, Booth, resigned almost immediately after the election and John George Barston assumed the vacancy. He was a lawyer born in Red River with a practice in Barkerville. These three represented Cariboo until 1875.

Walkem was then returned but with A. E. B. Davie, John Evans and George Cowan. Alexander Edmund Batson Davie had been born in Somerset, England in 1847, admitted as an attorney of British Columbia in 1868, and called to the bar of this province in 1873. George Cowan was elected in his stead. Davie's later importance in the political sphere came in a different constituency. Cowan, an Ontarian who came to British Columbia from Australia's gold mines in 1862, for many years had mining interest with his uncle, James Reid. Cowan made his home in Barkerville, won a by-election in 1877 and continued to represent the riding until 1890. John Evans, a Welshman, led the group of Welsh miners to Cariboo, and though he was a mining surveyor by profession, his mining ventures were unsuccessful. His is the story of disappointment after disappointment, of borrowing money year after year, and of writing to his family that "this time," certainly, he would strike pay dirt. When he died in 1879 he still had not done so. Although a candidate in the first election, he was unsuccessful until 1875; he was returned in 1878 as an Independent. On Evans's death, George Ferguson was elected, but in spite of his popularity as a miner, he went down to defeat in 1886 when the Liberal movement was becoming powerful.

Walkem did not contest the election of 1882, for he had been made a judge. Charles Wilson and Robert McLeese represented Cariboo at Victoria with Ferguson. McLeese of Soda Creek was descended from an old Scottish family which had settled in County Antrim, Ireland, in 1828. He came to Canada in the early 1860s. In 1862, he was Chief Engineer with the New Westminster Fire Department, but went to Cariboo in search of gold. However, he began to farm at Soda Creek, had a store, was postmaster, owned the steamboat *Victoria* and operated a hotel. In 1886 he again went to the capital, this time with Cowan and Joseph Mason. Mason was an Englishman who settled in Barkerville in 1866 as a general merchant with mining interests. Re-elected in the next election, he died in 1891. He was succeeded by Ithiel Blake Nason, a "State-of-Mainer" living in British Columbia since 1858, a sawmill owner and gold miner as well as trustee of the Royal Cariboo Hospital and of the Barkerville school. Nason died in 1893 and William Adams of Lightning Creek was sent in his place. He was a farmer and stock raiser who had come from Dumfries, Ontario. With Adams, John Robson and Samuel Augustus Rogers represented the riding. Robson, from Ontario, had come west in 1859, had established the New Westminster *British Columbian*, and as Cabinet Minister had represented New Westminster. Robson died in 1982 and Dr. Watt was his successor.

The census of 1891 showed a declining population in Cariboo, and following a redistribution the district henceforth had only two seats. At the election three years later, Major General J. C. Kinchant was defeated and Cariboo sent Adams and Rogers. Samuel Augustus Rogers had earned respect as Sheriff of the district. At the time of his election he was a merchant and notary public as well as a director of the hospital at Barkerville. Kinchant was elected in 1898 and sat for the constituency with Hans Helgeson who had been with the second group of prospectors on the Horsefly River in 1859 and who died at Metchosin in 1918, at the age of 87. In 1900 Hunter and Rogers were again elected.

In the election of 1903 Harry Jones, having lost the election of 1900, successfully contested the seat as a Liberal. He had come to Cariboo from Wales after the peak of the great gold excitement and lived there until his death in 1936. This election was an important occasion, and the riding for the first time elected a "native son." James Murphy, son of Denis Murphy, had been born at 141 Mile House in 1872, educated at St. Joseph's Mission at Williams Lake and later, in law, at Ottawa University. He was a Liberal. From 1907 to 1909 Harry Jones sat with another Liberal, John MacKay Yorston. Born in the Orkney Islands in 1867, Yorston had come to Canada in 1890 and freighted on the Great North Road. In 1903, after he and his brother Robert purchased the Australian Ranch, he began to farm. During his freighting years, he was extremely popular and later, while farming, won respect through his progressive ideas and reliability. The Liberals of Cariboo were ousted in 1909 when the Federal party lost favour, and Yorston was not re-elected until 1916.

When Yorston was defeated, John Anderson Fraser of Quesnel became Member of the Legislative Assembly along with Michael Callanan, an Irish physician at the Barkerville hospital. Both these Conservatives represented Cariboo until 1916. Fraser had gone to Quesnel to teach school but shortly went to work for Senator Reid. Leaving the Reid Estate to start his own store, Fraser became interested in the Northern Interior Printing Company which published the *Cariboo Observer*. Naturally, the newspaper supported him.

Before World War I the Conservatives rode the crest of a prosperity wave until faced with a depression in 1913. At this time the Conservative provincial government was promoting the Pacific Great Eastern Railway. When Richard McBride, the party leader, announced that the railway had to be finished, the party split. McBride was replaced by William John Bowser who said that no money would be spent on the railway. In that election of 1916, Cariboo, now with only one member, watched the contest between two favourites, John A. Fraser and John M. Yorston. The choice was difficult for Quesnel people, but hoping that the Pacific Great Eastern would be completed they returned the Liberal, Yorston. The *Cariboo Observer* had backed the losing Fraser; Yorston continued to represent Cariboo until 1923. Then General McRae traded on post-war disillusionment and advanced his Provincial Party; Cariboo elected McRae's candidate, D. A. Stoddart of Clinton who defeated both Yorston and Fraser and represented the riding until 1928. A retired stock raiser, he had represented Lillooet from 1890 to 1895.

When Premier "Honest John" Oliver died, the Liberals lost their leader. The Opposition leader, Simon Fraser Tolmie, was popular and in the election of 1928, when the Conservatives swept the province, Cariboo elected the prosperous merchant from Williams Lake, Roderick Mackenzie. The southern sector of the constituency thus took on the political leadership. R. N. Campbell, a Liberal from Horsefly, and D. A. Stoddart, by this time an Independent, ran against Mackenzie. But Tolmie's party assumed the reins of government just when the world went into its greatest depression, and the province blamed all its troubles on the Conservative government. In 1933 the riding sent a land surveyor from Williams Lake, Donald MacKay, to swell the ranks of the Liberal party. At this election the C.C.F. party appeared for the first time with R. W. Haggen as candidate.

At the 1937 polls Louis LeBourdais of Quesnel was chosen. He had reluctantly accepted nomination, but became the most colourful member in the Legislative Assembly as he furthered agricultural interests in Cariboo and brought his district to the attention of the entire Dominion of Canada. Born in Clinton, he had moved to Quesnel to become telegraph operator and later an insurance salesman. A local historian, he has become a legend in the community. R. N. Campbell expressed the sentiment of the riding when he threw his support to LeBourdais at the Liberal meeting of 1941: "Louis LeBourdais is Grade A1 whether on the hoof or rail." Without any doubt, he was the most popular member ever elected in Cariboo (he held his seat until he died in 1947) as a civilian and as a soldier, as a Liberal and as a Coalitionist.

Walter Hogg of Kamloops filled the vacancy made by the death of LeBourdais, and, like every other Cariboo candidate in the past, condemned the roads. He held the seat for a year, and died in September 1949. Angus MacLean, a Coalitionist from Wells, won the seat in 1949, but was defeated in 1952 by Ralph Chetwynd of the new Social Credit party. Chetwynd retained the seat with cabinet appointments until he died in 1957. The seat was then vacant until William C. Speare, the hospital administrator and a Social Credit candidate, was elected in September of that year.

In 1871 British Columbia as a Canadian province elected members to the Federal House of Commons. The first Member of Parliament from Cariboo was sent by acclamation: Joshua Spencer Thompson, an editor of Barkerville's *Cariboo Sentinel*, a paper which had been a great advocate of Confederation. He was returned four times, but died in 1880 before his last term expired. James Reid of Quesnel succeeded him.

A native of Hull, Quebec, Reid had first passed through

Quesnel in 1862 on his way to the mines, but moved to the junction settlement in 1873 where he opened a store with Hibbard Hudson and soon had the largest mercantile business in the town. He became president of the Hixon Creek Gold Quartz Company and, at the time of his death in 1905, owned a store, a sawmill and a flour mill in the town as well as the Steamer *Charlotte* which plied the river. A Conservative, he became a Senator in 1888.

James Reid was succeeded in the House of Commons by Frank Stillman Barnard, another supporter of the John A. Macdonald administration. Barnard had been born in Ontario in 1856 and came to British Columbia in 1860, a year after his father, Francis J. Barnard, who founded the British Columbia Express Company. In 1880 young Barnard was appointed manager of the "B.X," but resigned to contest the Cariboo riding which he represented until 1896, in spite of his unpopularity for being associated with the great "Cariboo Octopus," the B.C. Express.

That year, 1896, the Yale-Cariboo riding, which included the vast Kootenay district, elected Hewitt Bostock, a Liberal, who was defeated in 1900 by W. A. Galliher, the representative until 1903. "Kootenay" was carved from Yale-Cariboo in 1903, and Galliher was elected to represent the new riding, while his friend Duncan Ross defeated Martin Burrell in the old one. The constituency had elected Liberals since 1896, but in 1908 Liberal popularity was waning and Yale-Cariboo elected the Conservative Burrell. He was re-elected in the Conservative landslide of 1911 and remained in office until 1917.

The redistribution in 1914 allowed Cariboo once more to choose a member for itself in the election of 1917 when women had a vote. Widows, wives, mothers and sisters of soldiers voted for the first time along with the men to continue the war-time coalition under Robert Borden: Cariboo elected Frederick John Fulton of Kamloops. The usual desire for a change of parties following a war defeated Fulton in 1921 and elected T. G. McBride, a Progressive.

Without a local figure in the limelight, the Quesnel region had become less interested in federal politics. In 1925, however, John Anderson Fraser, a Conservative, was elected. A leader of the town both socially and politically since his arrival, in 1909 he had been elected to the Legislative Assembly. Following his defeat in 1916 he had worked behind the political scenes and emerged in the federal sphere. Fraser's position during his ten years as Member of Parliament was not an enviable one. For five years, as a Conservative in a predominantly Liberal House led by Prime Minister W. L. Mackenzie King, Fraser was ineffectual. During the period when R. B. Bennett was Premier, Canada was hurt by the great depression, and Cariboo with the rest of the world was held in its grip.

In 1935, again ready for a change of government and hoping for better times, but not blaming Fraser, Cariboo returned J. G. Turgeon, a Liberal, who was not defeated until 1945, when a former Albertan, W. Irvine, of the Co-operative Commonwealth Federation, was sent to Ottawa. Turgeon was appointed to the Senate on January 27, 1947. Irvine met problems similar to those met by Fraser from 1925 to 1930. The constituency returned George Matheson Murray, a Liberal from Fort St. John in 1949. He was defeated in 1953 by Bert Raymond Leboe, a Social Crediter from McBride, who was in turn defeated in the 1958 Progressive Conservative sweep by W. G. Henderson of Rolla.

CHAPTER TWELVE

Roads to Cariboo

The discovey of rich gold-bearing creeks in Cariboo brought about the construction of the Cariboo Road. Governor Douglas recognized the necessity for a road to carry supplies into the "diggings," for without one no miners would enter the region. He also realized that mining is a forerunner of colonization, and that permanent settlers require a thoroughfare. Settlement had already started in the Fraser Valley, and before 1860 farmers were locating at far-away Beaver Lake and Quesnelmouth. Barkerville with its gold was 600 miles away, either by way of the Fraser River to Hope by steamer and on to Lillooet or along the Harrison-Anderson Lake route by raft, canoe or on foot. During August and September 1858, Royal Engineers, with voluntary labour on the part of the miners, started building the Harrison-Anderson Lake road and trail in order to permit entry to the Fraser north of the Yale canyon, the "almost insurmountable barrier" that Fraser had noted. However satisfactory this route may have been, it was inadequate: the exceedingly rich gold bars between Yale and Lytton were isolated. In August of the same year Douglas allotted money to construct a mule track following the old Hudson's Bay Company brigade trail. Cut by Franklin Way, who later moved farther north, the trail was useful four months of the year. In the meantime, in 1861 the Harrison-Lillooet route was finished.

In 1862 a delegation waited for Governor Douglas to discuss

the building of a wagon road along the Fraser to Lytton and Cook's ferry, now known as Spence's Bridge. Royal Engineers then surveyed from Yale to Boston Bar and from Lytton to the ferry; the stretch between Boston Bar and Lytton was contracted, and Sgt. McColl selected a site for bridging the Fraser. The following year Capt. J. Grant, with the Engineers, worked on the section from Yale to Pike's Riffle, and Thomas Spence built from there to Chapman's Bar under contract. Joseph Trutch constructed the next twelve miles to Boston Bar, and Spence from Boston Bar to Lytton, these sections being built concurrently. In the summer of 1863 four hundred men worked on the last section alone. In fact, although the contracts were let separately, Spence and Trutch were partners. In March of 1862 Charles Oppenheimer and Walter Moberly contracted for the road between Lytton and the ferry and advertised for one thousand men. Because gold lured so many men away from road construction, the contractors had had to hire Indians and Chinese, but then a smallpox epidemic reduced this source of labour. The government demanded more speed and, when the contractors could not meet the demands, cancelled the contract and finished the section late in the year with miners who had come out from the diggings for the winter and were looking for work. Moberly was retained and took charge for the government.

Gustavus Blin Wright built forty-seven miles from Lillooet to Cut-Off Valley, or Clinton, and on August 16, 1862 obtained the contract to finish the road from Lillooet to Alexandria. It was usable to Soda Creek by the end of July the following year. The month that the road reached Soda Creek, so did the first stage coach.

Trutch constructed the bridge across the Fraser in 1863; it was named Alexandra Bridge for the Princess Royal. The connecting link between Cook's Ferry and the existing Lillooet-Alexandria road was then built, the first nine miles by Royal Engineers and the remainder by William Hood, an American located at Cache Creek. In 1864 Spence undertook to erect a bridge to replace Cook's ferry, and although his attempt was considerably damaged by a freshet, he completed the crossing that fall and collected tolls for over two years in order to recoup his losses.

The road was financed in two ways: portions built by Royal Engineers for the Colonial government were paid from the colonial allowance, the remainder by cash and bonds. Tolls payable to the contractors were charged at Alexandra and Spence's bridges, and on the road north from Lillooet, which became known as "Mile 0." These tolls were the source of annoyance for years and were used as planks in political platforms until the last toll was removed in 1951 when the one on the Patullo Bridge was eliminated.

This government-sponsored road was not the only one suggested. The gold fields of Cariboo invited speculators of all types. Various routes to the mines were promoted, one of them by way of Bentinck Arm to the Fraser, along the West Road River, following Mackenzie's early route. Alfred Waddington hoped to retain the centre of trade in Victoria and feared the centre would move to the lower Fraser River towns. He wanted to run steam communication between Victoria and Bute Inlet to connect with a wagon road through the Chilcotin to Quesnel.

The government was interested in the shortest, best and least expensive route, and sent Lt. H. Spencer Palmer of the Royal Engineers to explore the Bentinck Arm trail in the summer of 1862. The Fraser River road was already being constructed north from Lillooet, but was opposed by people with interests elsewhere. Palmer's report reduced criticism of the Fraser road when he found that although the Chilcotin route was about equidistant from Lillooet and of an easy gradient with small timber for corduroying, it had many slides, and pasturage only on the last fifty miles to Alexandria. The government's Cariboo Road had good pasturage and was capable of producing hay and grain. In his report of November 24, 1862 to Col. R. C. Moody, Palmer included this statement:

...the Bentinck Arm route is, from its high continuous elevation and from the general absence of good soil in the district which it traverses, unlikely, for the present at least, to acquire importance as an arterial highway to the established gold mines of this country.

In spite of the report, Waddington persisted in his attempt to build the Bentinck Arm road, but in 1864 Indians massacred his men. (Some of the Indians were later hanged at Quesnel.)

Palmer also explored two routes from Williams Lake to the mines: one through Beaver Lake and Quesnel Forks, "the eastern route," as he called it, and one through Alexandria and the mouth of the Quesnel to Cottonwood, "the western route." In a report to Moody dated February 21, 1863, Palmer advocated the western roadway:

> Regarding Richfield as the centre of the present gold district, for its supply I give preference to the western route, for although it is about 149 miles from the head of Williams Lake to Richfield by the Cottonwood trail, and but 113 by way of the forks of Quesnel River, the extra distance in the former case is, I consider, more than compensated by the superior character of the trails in the latter, and by the quantity and quality of the pasture which borders them.
>
> As an arterial highway through the colony, the western line, as far as the mouth of the Quesnel River, undoubtedly has the superiority. The ascertained north-westerly tendency of the gold-bearing ranges, each year becoming more apparent, the bent of the Cariboo mines in the same direction, and the reports of rich discoveries on the Peace river at once indicate the policy of adhering to the Fraser valley in the construction of the first main trunk-road, thus avoiding the mountainous country, and admitting the adoption of steam navigation in suitable places.

Above all, Palmer insisted, roads must be constructed. Eager miners must have access to the gold and they were being discouraged by the abominably bad trails. Trails of a sort did lead from Williams Lake and Alexandria to Quesnel Forks and the mines, and there were trails from the mouth of the Quesnel, all formerly used by animals, Indians, and Hudson's Bay Company couriers. Early government officials, too, hired men to cut through the bush. In May 1862 Gold Commissioner Elwyn let a contract for a trail four feet wide from MacDonald's Bar to where Van Winkle Creek joins Lightning Creek. Completed by June 15, 1862 the trail cost 250. Palmer really did not distinguish one type of trail from another when he reported on their condition:

> It is difficult to find language to express in adequate terms the utter vileness of the trails of Cariboo, dreaded alike by all classes of travellers; slippery, precipitous ascents and descents, fallen logs, overhanging branches, roots, rocks, swamps, turbid pools and miles of deep mud. . . . The only good parts are on the actual summits of the bald hills; even the upper portions of the slopes are, in many places, green, spongy swamps, the head waters of the radiating creeks; and, directly the forest is entered, the more serious evils begin.

Even before Palmer submitted his report, Moody had seen the advisability of the western route. In January 1862 tenders were called for a wagon road 18 feet wide from Alexandria through Quesnelmouth to Van Winkle, and for a bridle road from there to Richfield and to Antler. Because moving Royal Engineers northward would be too costly, the road was contracted, but tenders came slowly. Eventually Capt. Grant drew a contract for Allen Smith to build a trail 10 feet wide, suitable in winter for sleighing from Quesnelmouth to Van Winkle. By mid-July it was finished to Swift River; by September, through Van Winkle. An 8 foot bridle trail led from there to Williams Creek. That winter G. B. Wright was sleighing goods from Quesnel to Cottonwood; in March 1864 his sleighs travelled all the way to Richfield over Smith's trail.

The road from Clinton to Alexandria built by Wright was in good condition, but Wright was not anxious that it should be continued farther. He owned the only means of transportation from Soda Creek, the Steamship *Enterprise*, and with Frank Way owned Deep Creek Ranch. The night steamer reached Soda Creek at such an hour that passengers could only travel a short distance down the road, as far as Deep Creek, before dark. From Soda Creek to the mouth of the Quesnel River a trail wound along the banks of the Fraser.

Nevertheless, sleighs followed courier and farmer trails across Alexandria prairie to Quesnel in January 1864. Tenders for building a road had been called in 1863, but not until the summer of 1865 was Robert T. Smith awarded the contract, under the inspectorship of Spence. Smith began work in July, paying his workers a flat rate of $70 a month and board, and by September had built to the Quesnel River which had to be crossed by ferry. Heavy wagons cut the road badly and the fall rains made it a mass of gumbo, but Smith had contracted to keep the road in good condition for one year. When he refused to do repair work, he forfeited his contract, and Spence then assumed the responsibility of keeping the road in condition for the government. The Deep Creek Farm stopping house then decreased in importance.

Before the road was built goods travelled from Soda Creek to Quesnel by steamer, but there was no wagon road from Quesnel to Richfield. In May 1864 Trutch surveyed one. Tenders did not come quickly, and the government deemed it advisable that the road should be built in sections and supervised by Walter Moberly. The contract for the lower section, from Quesnel to Cottonwood, was awarded to G. B. Wright for $85,000. Employing 520 men he boarded them all; choppers were paid $75 a month and graders $60. Included in the 520 men were 300 Chinese who were paid only $45 a month. Wright bridged the Cottonwood River under a separate contract for $9,000—the bridge was completed in November 1864—and that winter Allen Smith and John Ryder sleighed goods to Richfield. In the spring the firm of Humphry, Pool and Johnston operated a stage line from Quesnel to Cottonwood. Wright made an estimated profit of $40,000 on this road alone.

In April 1865, Malcolm Munro of Victoria secured the contract to construct the road from Cottonwood to Richfield and commenced at once in order to complete the work by October, for unless the road were finished the $45,000 contract would be annulled. Munro built to Van Winkle only to be defeated by bad weather. He wrote to Trutch, then Chief Commissioner of Lands and Works, asking for permission to furnish bond and to finish the road in the spring. Trutch refused. Munro owed about $8,000 to his employees and $5,000 to local merchants; he gave bills of sale for all his equipment to three people and then left the district, went to jail in New Westminster and, finally, ended in bankruptcy court. James Duncan finished the road on his own volition and billed the government for $509.63.

Naturally a cry arose on Williams Creek for a road from Richfield to Camerontown. This short route was surveyed by Spence and the contract awarded to Wright for the extremely low price of $6,700. Under the contract Wright built as far as Barkerville. To stop the road there was ridiculous, but Wright asked $900 to continue it through Barkerville to Camerontown. This town on Williams Creek raised $500 and Wright finished the road.

With the completion of the Williams Creek section, the road was open from Yale to the mines, virtually following the route as originally planned by Moberly, Spence and Grant, with advice in part from Palmer. Canadian Pacific Railway builders destroyed much of the original road through the canyons, and Canadian National Railway construction crews nearly completed the destruction. Not until 1926 was the road rebuilt.

One last section of road is of interest, as much for the legend surrounding it as for the sake of the road itself. The "river road" from Williams Creek to Soda Creek was built in 1932 in order to by-pass Carpenter Mountain. This section was planned by original surveyors and recommended by Lt. Palmer, but during construction Wright cut the road over the mountain instead of along the old brigade trail which followed the San Jose River and the Fraser banks. According to legend, when Wright had constructed the road from Clinton as far as the 140 Mile Post he applied for a loan to Thomas Manifee who ran an extremely good stopping house at Williams Lake. Manifee's refusal offended Wright.

Contractors were permitted to deviate from the surveys when they considered it practicable to do so. Wright built the road past the 150 Mile Post and over Carpenter's Mountain to Deep Creek, by-passing Williams Lake and, according to the story, taking revenge on Manifee for refusing the loan. However, before the road was built the government had agreed to the deviation. Nevertheless, Wright had an interest in Frank Way's stopping house, and a road through Williams Lake would have by-passed his own lucrative business.

A rumour of the time credited Way with having given Wright a half interest in Deep Creek Farm on the condition that Wright would build the road over Carpenter Mountain. The quarrel with Manifee might have been merely a "red herring." Teamsters said no feed existed over the river route and opposed later attempts to re-route the road. Because of this opposition, coupled with expense, the old road crossed the mountain until 1932, when a road then also followed the river. In 1953 a new road was built between these two. The new one also skirts Carpenter Mountain and goes within a half mile of the old Manifee place.

CHAPTER THIRTEEN

Modes of Transport

Up the great, new road went the people to the mines: the argonauts, the merchants, the card sharps, the swindlers, the policemen, the loggers, the swampers, the hurdy-gurdy girls, the saloon keepers, the government officials. Some walked leading Newfoundland dogs; the Olson brothers manoeuvred their trundle barrow with shafts fore and aft. Frank Laumeister's camels trekked to Cariboo on the completed road, but the feet of the beasts were unsuited for stony roads and rough, rock trails, unsuited for the intervals of marsh and mud, and mule "skinners" object to the stench of the strange-looking animals. Other pack animals became unmanageable when camels were nearby, accidents occurred, and litigation followed. Although one old timer said the animals were butchered and sold for beef, Laumeister decided, wisely, to turn the animals loose near the Thompson River, and the last survivor died about 1905 at Westwold.

Bull trains, too, were common on the great thoroughfare. William Rose, who later lived at Rose Lake, was one of the best with a black snake. Another was "Dirty Harry" Strouse, who had been trained for the priesthood. One of the most colourful drivers, he prodded his twelve yoke of oxen, hauling three wagon along the gravel highway, over the mountains and across the flats. The decrease in mining hastened the end of the bull trains because less heavy freight was required, and the horse and mule outfits forced the slow, stubborn oxen off the road.

The greatest of all packers was Jean Caux, better known as Cataline. Born in the Spanish province of Catalonia and having come to Cariboo in the early 1860s, Cataline rode at the head of a sixty-mule train which was followed by a white bell-mare. Through dust and dirt, he wore a large hat, blue overalls tucked into high cowboy boots, a frock coat, and always a white, stiff-fronted shirt. The shirt was a new one every trip and never left his back until the trek was over. His packing crew included Indians, Chinese, and an occasional Negro, but seldom a white man. His foreman was an aged Chinese.

No pack saddles were used on the Cariboo Road with its treacherous canyons. Rather than a pack saddle, a leather sack filled with hay or straw, an "aparajoe," was strapped tightly onto the back of a mule; onto this, 200 to 300 pounds of freight were lashed, held in place by diamond hitch, breast strap and crupper. No lead lines were used either. Mules walked freely so that one animal crashing to the river hundreds of feet below would not drag others after him. Rate of travel was about fifteen miles a day. A trip from Yale to the mines took a month, the return a little less; three trips were made a season. Early in 1861 the freight rate on goods was $1 a pound; improved roads reduced it to 40¢.

Of all the modes of transportation on the Cariboo Road, stage coaches were the most practical, the safest and the fastest. Competition was great, but eventually all fell before the might of Francis Jones Barnard. In 1858, "Billy" Ballou's Pioneer Fraser River Express ran to the diggings on the Lower Fraser and connected with Wells Fargo in Victoria. In 1859 Jeffray's Fraser River Express began and operated for two years when it sold to the Barnard outfit. That year, 1861, the Cariboo rush was developing rapidly. Ballou and Barnard operated opposition express companies, but because Barnard was too strong and too well backed "Billy" was forced to sell to Dietz and Nelson, who came to a working agreement with Barnard. Dietz and Nelson were to operate stage lines from Victoria to Yale by the Fraser route and to Lillooet by the Harrison route. At both places their stages connected with those of Barnard's Cariboo Express which ran to the mines. The arrangement lasted until 1867 when Barnard absorbed the Dietz and Nelson organization. Five years late the name of the company was changed to the F. J. Barnard Company. In 1879 Barnard retired and the huge organization became the British Columbia Express Company, "the B.X.," under Barnard's henchmen, Stephen Tingley and James Hamilton. A Toronto firm bought the company in 1896 and ran the last stages until 1913.

Barnard was born in Quebec in 1829 of American parents and came to British Columbia seeking gold in 1859, but had little success. He sold a claim he had staked at Yale in order to become constable. This position he resigned to become purser on the steamer *Yale*. When she exploded on the river he chopped wood and graded Douglas Street in Yale, before trudging to Cariboo on foot, delivering letters and selling newspapers. Each paper he sold for $1; for each letter delivered he collected $2. By 1862, in better financial condition, he purchased horses with which to operate a pony express. The ponies carried the load, but Barnard continued to walk. Because he was the colony's most trusted expressman he had not trouble obtaining deliveries, and accumulated money enough to expand his operations. Before the Cariboo Road was completed, Barnard bought wagons and harness in Victoria and employed Stephen Tingley to drive for him, so that when the road opened he was ready with Barnard's Express and Mail Lines from Lillooet to Soda Creek. The beginnings were small in 1863: a two-horse wagon rattled between Lillooet and Alexandria every ten days with Tingley holding the "ribbons."

Barnard's first real stage coach left Yale on March 12, 1864 at 5 a.m. with James Down driving, and from that time the company ran stages over the road to Cariboo. The hairpin curves of the canyon, the steep hills and sheer drops may have held terrors for the passengers, but the drivers swung onward from one road house to another. Four horses usually drew the stages, but where necessary six were used. On Alexandria Prairie, or wherever going was easy, only two horses were used if the load was light. A trip took about fifty hours from Yale to Soda Creek, and the fare was $130 each way. Meals at roadhouses were usually priced at 50¢; accommodation might be another 50¢. At the more northerly stopping houses, from Felker's "Blue Tent" northward, the price of a meal was generally 75¢. Special wagons carried most express, but occasionally the stages carried some. Charges for parcels were $1 a pound, if under 25 pounds, 90¢ if between 25 and 100 pounds, and 75¢ if over 100 pounds. Treasure in gold was carried in iron chests from the mines to Yale and shipped from there to Victoria by steamer.

In 1872 traffic had increased to such an extent that two stages were running weekly and fares were reduced to $65 for the trip from Yale to Quesnel, a trip of sixty hours. With the coming of the Canadian Pacific Railway and the destruction of the road through the Fraser Canyon, the express company established headquarters in Ashcroft in 1886. Staging from Ashcroft was neither so dangerous nor so exciting.

It is understandable that at first fares should be high. Feed was exceedingly costly, with hay prices ranging from $35 a ton at Yale to $350 a ton at Barkerville. Grain, horseshoes and other essentials cost as much proportionally. The best procurable horses were imported early from Oregon, but in 1868 Barnard sent Tingley to California to select 400 good mares and stallions and to bring them to the newly established B.X. Ranch, which was on the site of the present-day city of Vernon. There the best horses in British Columbia were bred. Eventually the band increased to 2,000 head and from them the stagers were chosen. These animals were never completely "broken," but trained for staging and staging alone; a broken horse, the company considered, was a spoiled horse. Because of their great value, horses received the best of care; when they showed signs of wear they were replaced. Good pastures and meadows were kept where jaded animals could rest and recuperate. About 250 horses were always at hand, while 150 were continually in harness. The stations were located about eighteen miles apart with fresh horses waiting at each one. At some stops the passengers had no time to climb from the coach: the team from the completed eighteen-mile lap was unhooked; new horses, fresh and lively, were swung into place, and hooked up. Off at a gallop for a few hundred yards, they settled to a steady trot to the next station. The change took only minutes.

Such an organization requires planning and enterprise. The Barnard outfit had both. The company maintained its own paint, wheelwright, repair and blacksmith shops, as well as travelling blacksmiths who could put a "hot" shoe on a horse right on the road in order to keep the stages moving. The coaches, Concord type, came first from California, but had to be so strengthened to meet local conditions that finally the company built its own. Stages and all other conveyances, of which there were many types, were in company colours: bodies of brilliant red, with gears and spokes of bright yellow.

Working for the Barnard Express made one an "aristocrat" of the road: employees were proud of their work and of their associates. Drivers, and expressmen, blacksmiths and hostlers, agents and clerks, all were proud of their connection. At Quesnel, G. Goudie was expressman until the stage began stopping in front of James Reid's store and Reid took over the work. Sellers and Dunlevy had the agency at Soda Creek, J. A. Newland the one at Barkerville. Wayne Huston, also of Soda Creek, was one of the crack drivers.

An efficient, dependable service, the "B.X." became a household by-word. Nevertheless, it was too great an organization to escape criticism, and some called it the "Cariboo Octopus." Opposition companies began, mostly by disaffected employees, but Barnard absorbed them. Criticism and opposition hurt little except in 1871 when the company lost the mail contract; but ten months later the B.X. was carrying the mails once more, the other group having failed to fulfill its contract. Tingley and Hamilton became partners in the company in 1872, and in 1888 Tingley, who had been associated with Barnard from the outset, bought the shares held by Barnard and his son and became sole owner of the property.

In 1896, with a change of government, the company again lost the mail contract. In order to fulfill his contract Charles V. Millar, a Toronto lawyer, had to purchase the company to acquire coaches, wagons, harness, horses and other equipment. Mail service under the new owners commenced on July 1, 1897. With the proposed construction of the Grand Trunk Pacific Railway into Prince George and the subsequent land boom bringing a rush of people to the northern Cariboo, extra stages ran from Ashcroft, and the B.X. expanded its steamer trade to carry the people up the river north of Quesnel.

The day of coaching was almost over with the advent of the automobile. The first one to arrive in Cariboo came in June 1907, a McLaughlin-Buick owned by O. P. Perry of the Bullion Mine and driven by Alexander Stevenson. But this was not the first attempt to operate motors on the highway—it was merely the mark that they were successful. In 1871 F. J. Barnard and J. C. Beedy of Van

Winkle had tried to use two of R. W. Thompson's "Patent India Rubber Tire Road Steamers" specially fitted for mail and express, but because they were not suited to the rough, winding roads, they ended their careers on Jackass Mountain during their first trip from Yale.

Little did the stage driver realized when he met that first car at La La Hache that it signified the end of an era. The B.C. Express Company, having to augment its horses with automobiles, bought two Winton Sixes at Seattle, shipped them to Vancouver by boat and to Ashcroft by rail, and painted them the famous company colours, red and yellow. The automobiles were not profitable, but competition had to be met. Heavy freight wagons cut deep ruts in the gravel roads and these ruts filled with mud and rocks. The narrow tires of the automobiles then dug into the ruts, and the cars settled into the mud to the running boards, often damaging them badly. The B.C. Express Company eventually used eight of these cars and costs rose. When the mail contract was lost in 1913, the company sold the cars and staging equipment to the new mail contractors, Mayor J. T. Robinson of Kamloops and J. C. Shields of Vancouver. Millar's company retained the steamers, and when the new contractors failed, the B.X., for $500 a week, guaranteed to carry the mail for them from Soda Creek to Fort George by steamer. With the coming of the war, freighting on the road came to an abrupt standstill, but the B.X. carried the mails until October 1915. The company steamer *B.X.* was damaged in 1919, but the *B.C. Express* plied the Fraser until 1920. The tying up and dismantling of the *B.C. Express* ended the operations of a great company which had been transporting men and goods for sixty years.

The B.X. was one of the last stage lines in North America. The automobile spelled its doom. Before long, automobiles crossed the Fraser by ferry at Quesnel and, following G. B. Wright's road along the Blackwater, travelled to Prince George. Early freighters, like the Yorston brothers and George Duclos, retired early enough to prosper as farmers or roadworkers. Freighting had demanded feed for horses and for men, and had demanded roadwork and services. James Craig arrived in Quesnel to work on the road in 1876. Joseph St. Laurent, married in Barkerville to Georgina Wilhelmina Henrietta Nachtingall, became the first foreman on the Cariboo Road.

Harry Moffat is a good example of a freighter-turned-farmer who also worked on the roads. At Alexandria he established his Lansdown Farm in 1883 and there ran a stopping house for freighters, supplying meals and lodging and facilities for changing stage horses. Some time later he became road superintendent from Fort George to 150 Mile, to Barkerville in the east and to Chilcotin in the west. He travelled this huge district with a two-wheeled cart pulled by one horse, in the early years even distributing the wages which were paid in cash.

At that time snow ploughs were rarely used, and the deep snow in Devil's Canyon necessitated the unloading of the big sleighs at Cottonwood and the transferring of goods and passengers to smaller sleighs for the remaining distance to Barkerville and back to Cottonwood. Harry Moffat designed a snow roller which was used on this section of the road for at least sixteen years and which enabled the larger sleighs to make the complete trip.

The staging road gave way to the auto road; by 1909 the stages were almost gone. Although George Johnston started a livery stable in 1909, A. E. Boyd had already established an auto repair shop; the Johnston brothers soon built a garage. Only freighters needed livery stables, and the much-touted railway would completely finish freighting. New cars appeared on the roads, new transportation companies like that of Norman Glover and Clarence Stevenson; but even they could not compete when the great buses eventually rolled over the highway into Quesnel.

CHAPTER FOURTEEN

Steamboats

Early travel on the Fraser River was by canoe or Hudson's Bay Company batteau. Such transport the miners used going north; in the fall of 1859, twenty or thirty boats were built to bring men down river. This mode of travel continued for some time, and though steam boats were operating from Soda Creek by October 1863, men were still running the river, as many as twenty in a batteau. One group left Quesnel on the 14th of October and four days later were at Yale; the fare was $25. The next year small boats ran from Quesnel to Soda Creek for a $6 fare. By this time one of the most fascinating parts of the trip to the mines had been inaugurated: the whistle of the steamboat could be heard coming around the Red Bluff bend into Quesnel. The river steamers plied the upper Fraser from 1863 until 1921.

In May 1863 the steamer *Enterprise* was launched to ply the river from Soda Creek to Quesnel. During the winter of 1862–63, at Four Mile Creek near Alexandria, she had been built by James Trahey for Capt. Thomas Wright in conjunction with Gustavus Blin Wright, the road builder. The engines and boilers were carried over the Harrison-Lillooet route by mule. This steamer, with a carrying capacity of 75 tons, was the lightest draft of any steamer in British Columbia. She was 110 feet long and 20 feet wide with 12-inch by 36-inch engines working to 60 horsepower; her two boilers were 36 inches in diameter, 10 feet long, and the diameter of the sternwheel was 15 feet 6 inches.

On her first trip, commanded by Thomas Wright, she left Alexandria at 4 p.m. on May 9, and arrived at Quesnel at 4 p.m. on the 10th, where she landed at the slip prepared for her. The return trip required only two hours and forty minutes from Quesnel to Alexandria, and from there to Soda Creek, one hour and twenty minutes. Freight charges for that distance were $40 a ton; fares were $7 for man or animal. The *Enterprise* normally left for Quesnel from Soda Creek on Monday, Wednesday and Friday, and returned the following days. W. G. Doane soon succeeded Thomas Wright as Captain.

Dr. Cheadle and Viscount Milton, probably the first tourists in Cariboo, rode on the *Enterprise*. They had come from England to walk across Canada, and on October 15, 1863 arrived at Soda Creek. The next day they took the steamer north:

> Steamer came in about 2 o'clock bringing a host of miners 2 of whom were very drunk and continued to imbibe every 5 minutes; during the time we stayed in the house they must have had 20 drinks. The swearing was something fearful. After we had been on board a short time the Captain, finding out who we were, gave us the use of his cabin, a comfortable little room & supplied us with cigars & a decanter of cocktail, also books & papers. We were fetched out every few minutes to have a drink with some one, the Captain taking the lead by standing champagne all round. We had some dozen to do before supper; no one the least affected, Milton & I shirking in quantity. The 'Cap' told us the boat was built on the river, all the timber sawn by hand, the shaft in 5 pieces packed on mules, cylinders in two, boiler plates brought in same manner. Boat cost $75,000!

> SATURDAY, OCT. 17th. As we did not leave Soda Creek until 4 & the boat makes very slow progress against the powerful current, we had to anchor for night after doing only some 10 miles. At daybreak we went 4 or 5 miles & then delayed by the dense fogs which prevail on the river in the early morning at this season. Passed Fort Alexander [sic] about 10. No great trade there now; depot of furs from the north; 20 miles from Soda Creek. Country more level & under usual Fraser benches, & low wooded hills; river banks sandy; few rocks; River about size of Saskatchewan at Edmonton; Coal found on banks. Continually called out to have a drink.

SUNDAY, OCT. 18th. Arrived about 9, at Quesnel mouth, a little collection of about 20 houses on the wooded banks of the Fraser. Quesnel at the north side of the Fort. Large new store & cards all lying about in the street....Captain Done [Doane] met us in street half seas over & insisted to treat us to champagne, etc., at every bar in the place.

On their return from the mines the two Englishmen found some gum boots in Beaver Pass and were able to walk through the mud to Quesnel. They could not wait for the steamer, which had been hauled onto shore for repairs, but instead arranged to travel to Soda Creek in a rowboat. Although not travelling aboard the *Enterprise*, Milton and Cheadle did visit Captain Doane, on November 4th:

Called on Captain Done [Doane] on the Steamer. Cocktails every 5 minutes, champagne lunch afterwards. Happiest man I ever saw. Steward tells me he takes a cocktail every ten minutes when on board. Very jolly fellow. Had to give a keg of brandy to his men before they could haul the steamer on shore. Gave them champagne dinner on being paid off today, & we heard them singing away below deck.

While travelling by rowboat, the two men had discovered that when the steamer transported chests of gold down river, an empty cask was attached to the chest by a long rope. If the steamer sank, the floating cask would show the location of the chest of gold.

In 1871, during the Omineca gold excitement, the *Enterprise* went through the canyons, up the Nechako River, the Stuart and Tachie rivers to Trembleur Lake and thence to Takla Landing by way of Middle River. G. B. Wright hoped to establish a speedy service to those northern gold fields, but the *Enterprise* made no return voyage, for the season was too short and by the time she arrived the overland route was in use. The *Enterprise* remained on Takla Lake.

In 1868, to handle the increased traffic going to Omineca, G. B. Wright and Edgar Marvin of Victoria had James Trahey build a sternwheeler, the *Victoria*, 116 feet long, 24 feet wide and 4 feet deep, with engines from the Lillooet Lake steamer *Prince of Wales*. They were 14 inches by 54 inches and capable of producing 90 horsepower; the diameter of the sternwheel was 17 feet 8 inches. Launched in 1869 she steamed from Soda Creek to Quesnel in eleven hours. When the *Enterprise* went to more northerly waters, the *Victoria* ran to the Cottonwood Canyon. In 1879 she was bought by Capt. John Irving, who had steamboat interests on the Lower Fraser, and his partner, Robert McLeese, merchant and hotel keeper at Soda Creek. In the fall of 1886 she was hauled from the river at Alexandria's steamboat landing, her days of service ended.

For ten years the river was without a steamboat, but in June 1896 the Northern British Columbia Navigation Company Limited, formed by Senator James Reid, Stephen Tingley and Capt. John Irving, laid the hull of a new ship under the supervision of Alexander Watson of Victoria, and on August 3, 1896 Mrs. Reid christened the steamer *Charlotte*, so named in her own honour. This superior river boat, 111.4 feet long, 20.6 feet in beam, with 11-inch by 60-inch cylinders working steam pressure of 160 pounds, was commanded by Frank Odin, with James McArthur as engineer. The initial run to Soda Creek from Quesnel was not made until October, very late in the busy year. On her last trip north from Soda Creek, the *Charlotte* forced her way through floating ice to reach Steamboat Landing, and because ice was running too heavily, the Captain was forced to tie up. The *Charlotte* became frozen in the river, and obviously had to be berthed there for the winter, out of the path of the destructive spring flow of ice, but directly in front of the new and glistening *Charlotte* lay the old *Victoria*. The owners of the *Charlotte* purchased the *Victoria* from McLeese and demolished her to make room for their own steamer. During World War I, the brass was stripped from the old *Victoria* and shipped for war material.

Within a few years, when the railway boom in the Fort George area attracted attention, both mail and goods had to pass through Quesnel. The British Columbia Express Company prepared to build a new boat to run north and the British Northern Navigation Company decided to inaugurate runs to the construction town with the *Charlotte*. She was given an overhauling, her cylinders sent to Victoria for a rebore, and a steam capstan installed on her forward deck so she could be lined up the strong currents. The pilot was Capt. O. F. Browne who had then been on the *Charlotte* for two years. In the summer of 1908, loaded with cordwood for fuel, she steamed to the foot of Cottonwood Canyon. A ring bolt had been fixed on the canyon wall and through it a cable was run from the capstan. Pulling herself through the treacherous canyon, the *Char-*

lotte had just reached the top when the ring bolt gave away and she crashed downstream, saved only by the efficient manoeuvring of her captain. She eventually made three trips through that year.

In January 1909 the *Cariboo Observer* announced that a local store keeper and fur trader, Telesphore Marion, was having John Strand of Quesnel build a steamer. The 70-feet by 16.2 feet *Quesnel*, with engines from Goderich, Ontario, was launched that year. A light boat using local coal, she had great carrying capacity.

That same year, 1909, Nick S. Clark, seeing the building boom of Fort George coming in the van of the railway, organized the Fort George Lumber and Navigation Company for whom Donald McPhee laid the keel of a new 70-foot river steamer, the *Nechacco*, at Quesnel. After being launched, and commanded by Capt. Bonser, she was drawn through the canyons and went almost to Fort St. James before returning to Soda Creek. That fall she carried six tons of supplies beyond Fort George for the rapidly approaching railway, and returning carried horses, oats and potatoes. The able and useful *Nechacco*, renamed the *Chilco* in 1910 because of registry requirements, did not last long—she was claimed by Cottonwood Canyon in May, 1911.

After Capt. Browne nearly lost the *Charlotte* in Cottonwood Canyon, he suggested that the federal government blast that dangerous rock obstacle. That winter, 1908 and 1909, the government did so. With this work done, and because of further economic advances to the north, the British Columbia Express Company entered the river boat service with the ''queen of the Upper Fraser,'' the *B.X.*, designed and built by Alexander Watson Jr., son of the designer and builder of the *Charlotte*. The hull was of local fir, but to reduce weight the housework above the main deck was of cedar freighted up the Cariboo Road from the coast. About fifty men worked on the new boat at Soda Creek in February 1910.

While the *B.X.* was being constructed, the Fort George Lumber and Navigation Company erected a shipyard on the beach, just downstream from the *B.X.* operation, where they build the small sternwheel prospecting boat *Fort Fraser*, as well as the large freight and passenger ship *Chilcotin*. During construction the crew working lower down river started the rumour that the *B.X.* was too wide to pass through the canyons above, and she promptly because known as the ''White Elephant.''

Ice jams at Soda Creek canyon backed up and damaged the *B.X.* hull but only a week was lost and Lloyd's of London, who had insured construction, paid the full loss. On May 23, 1910, the *B.X.* was ready to leave the river bank on her first voyage. Designed especially for carrying loads upstream, she was 127.5 feet long with a 28.8-foot beam and an all-over length of 150 feet, the sternwheel being 18 feet in diameter. The gross tonnage was 513.7. She had three decks with stateroom accommodation for 70 saloon passengers and a licence to carry 60 on deck, or 130 in all. At first she went only from Soda Creek to Quesnel, but on June 23, 1910, with Capt. Browne, formerly of the *Charlotte*, she left Quesnel for Fort George at 1 p.m. carrying 40 passengers and a load of freight. She reached Fort George at 4:30 p.m. the next day. The *Cariboo Observer* of May 28, 1910, praised her accommodations:

> Each stateroom has two berths with the exception of the beautiful bridal chamber. In each stateroom are stationery and wash stands, electric push buttons and reading lights. In the after part of the vessel is a bathroom with a porcelain tub and nickel fittings. The steamer will be heated throughout with steam heat, including radiators in each separate stateroom, an excellent provision for the cold months; and electric fans will cool the vessel in the warm summer days.

> The hangings of the staterooms and social halls are of a delicate green on this luxuriant steamer, and all upholstering of red car plush. The crockery, blankets and linens were all made especially for service on the "B.X." and are individually marked with the "B.X." monogram. Even the toilet soap is marked distinctly in the same manner. The house flag is of red and yellow, the company's colors, and the insignia combined of X. and C. is in the centre.

The "White Elephant" was a decided success while the *Chilcotin* was sadly underpowered, and tied up at Prince George for the summer. During this busy year on the river most steamers paid a profit; losses were great when a boat missed a trip for any reason.

Early in 1910 the *Charlotte* struck a reef in Fort George Canyon and because of her age, after being salvaged, she was left on the banks of the river at Quesnel where she later burned. The *Charlotte's* boiler was 26 feet long and 6 feet in diameter and weighed 20,000 pounds. Lulu Hautier had used Steve Tingley's sixteen-mule team to haul it from Ashcroft. The trip had taken six weeks, and the load was so great that the wheels 'dished' several times. The old boiler was used for twenty-five years and after being employed in a sawmill and then rusting for some years was sold in 1933 to Cariboo Gold Quartz at Wells for heating purposes.

In November 1910 the *Chilco* struck a rock six miles above the West Road River and was beached, partly submerged. In the spring Capt. George Ritchie attempted to float her out too early, and struck solid ice in the Cottonwood Canyon. The crew escaped, but the *Chilco* capsized, disappeared, and no trace was ever seen of her again on the river.

With the *Charlotte* and *Chilco* gone, there remained only the *Chilcotin*, the *Quesnel* and the *B.X.* In 1912 Alexander Watson Jr. came again to Soda Creek to build another boat for the big company. This boat, the *B.C. Express*, was designed to haul from Tête Jaune Cache to Fort George. Except for two fewer staterooms and an un-covered sternwheel, she was almost identical in appearance to the *B.X.* On July 1st the *B.C. Express*, under the commanded of Capt. Bucey, arrived at Quesnel from Soda Creek and continued on to Fort George, where she landed on July 4th.

With the coming of the railway to Fort George, haulage costs on goods coming by rail were cheaper than on goods coming by wagon from Ashcroft. Steamer service increased between Quesnel and Fort George. The *Fort Fraser*, from Fort George, was given a new shovel-nosed hull, and became known as the *Doctor*. After 1912 the *Quesnel* was used by her new owners, the Northern Trading Company. The *Conveyor* and *Operator*, both of Fort George, were running. At this time a depression which had hit Cariboo was rising to a climax. Most of the sternwheelers were hauled out of the river in 1914, but because the Express Company boats had to maintain the mail service, the *B.X.* remained and did most of the work. Even the *Quesnel* had not been paying. No boat ran in 1916 or 1917.

In 1918 the Quesnel Board of Trade appealed to the Provincial government for transportation in lieu of the promised railway, and the river service then became subsidized. In August 1919, while carrying cement to build Deep Creek bridge for the Pacific Great Eastern Railway, the construction work which would mean her own end, the *B.X.* filled with water and sank and, though salvaged at a cost of $40,000, did not run again. In her stead the *B.C. Express* was refitted. During the winter of 1920–21 both ships were dismantled, the equipment going to the Arctic Transportation Company of Alberta to be used on far-northern rivers, and the hulls left to rot on the river bank at South Fort George.

They had all disappeared but the *Quesnel*. In April 1921 Capt. D. A. Foster attempted to prove that steamboating was still practicable; together with W. H. Matheson he launched the *Quesnel* again. Three weeks later, carrying some passengers and a cargo consisting of a Ford car and 100 barrels of beer, the ship crashed onto the rocks of Fort George Canyon. After removing the cargo Matheson and Foster, with a gang of men, worked several months to free the ship from the rocks. They did so, but as she swung into the current, the steamer "capsized, sank, then came up again and dropped its boilers, engines and funnel, before disappearing forever." That was the end of the *Quesnel*. Hers was the last steamboat whistle to be heard on the Fraser.

CHAPTER FIFTEEN

The Pacific Great Eastern Railway

The land boom to the north of Quesnel in the first decade of this century was brought on by the building of the Grand Trunk Pacific Railway. In the fall of 1912 serious consideration was given to the construction of a north-south railway to tap the area along the Fraser. Before the construction of the Grand Trunk Pacific, the country north of the Canadian Pacific Railway was supplied from Ashcroft along the Cariboo Road. The main distributing point was Quesnel which was situated at the junction of road routes to the west, east, and south, and which was the trans-shipment centre for steamer transportation to the north. Prices were high in the area, so high that they discouraged settlers, so high that Boards of Trade and merchants of British Columbia contemplated building a railway from Prince George to Vancouver in order to reduce interior prices and thereby promote colonization. In 1912 Timothy Foley, Patrick Welsh and John Stewart contracted to build a railway between these two points.

This was neither the first nor the last of Cariboo's railway dreams. The Waddington plan had ended in disaster in 1864 when workers were massacred by Chilcotin Indians. Quesnel had hoped that the Grand Trunk Pacific would have gone south from Prince George through Quesnel to Squamish and Vancouver. In 1912 the Cariboo, Barkerville, and Willow Railway Company was organized for the purpose of constructing a line from the G.T.P. at Eagle Lake, following the Willow River to Barkerville and running extensions from there to Cunningham Creek, Quesnel Forks and Horsefly. The line was to cross the country to the Clearwater River and eventually to meet the Thompson River. This dream came to nothing.

The Pacific Great Eastern Railway was initiated primarily as a colonization road to the Peace River from Vancouver, and was to achieve international importance by meeting an Alaska railroad planned by the United States government. Foley, Welsh and Stewart incorporated a company to construct the 467-mile railway, and personally guaranteed to build, equip and operate the road which was to be completed by July 1, 1915. The sale of company shares was to finance the construction of the road, but the government also subsidized it at $35,000 a mile—later at $42,000 a mile. D'Arcy Tate was vice president and general counsel of the company which issued bonds for $20,160,000 and put up $40,000 itself. The $42,000-a-mile subsidy was to be raised by bonds and placed in a trust fund from which payments would be made in proportion to construction done. The Grand Trunk Pacific agreed that all freight, passengers, express and general traffic going to Vancouver and originating on its line would be rerouted onto the Pacific Great Eastern at Prince George where both railroad companies were to use the same station. Throughout the province enthusiasm for this venture knew no bounds and greatly exaggerated the boom of the period.

Construction commenced in 1912. The line was graded from Squamish almost to Prince George, but bridges north of the Chasm were not all completed; the section from North Vancouver to Whytecliffe was to operate within two years. In 1915 steel had been laid 120 miles from Squamish to Lillooet, and the next year Clinton had rails. But British Columbia's hopes were suddenly dashed when the company, having expended its fund, declared itself unable to complete the railroad or to operate the line already constructed. The trust fund which had been set up by the government to protect the province was exhausted. Building had proceeded without check by the government, which discovered that for one half the mileage the company had consumed the entire proceeds of the bond sale which was to pay $42,000-a-mile for the total distance.

British Columbia panicked. Rumours flew around of illegal contracts and irresponsible handling of trust fund monies and of excess profits made by promoters who had contributed inadequate amounts of capital themselves. Disclosures destroyed provincial faith in the project. The Conservative government of Premier Bowser, deeply involved financially, was ousted in an election and, in 1918, the new provincial government assumed the remaining shares of the company in order to protect itself from further losses.

In March 1918 the new Department of Railways cleared accumulated debris and slides from its newly acquired tracks and within three weeks operated a regular train from Squamish to Clinton. In July of that same year the new owners awarded a contract to Northern Construction Company which was to finish the line to Prince George on a cost plus basis. By 1919 the line operated to Lone Butte and by 1920 to Williams Lake, a settlement revitalized after being almost non-existent since 1863 when G. B. Wright by-passed it with the road over Carpenter Mountain. In October 1921 the first train ran from Squamish to Quesnel.

Northward from Quesnel track was laid to the Cottonwood River in order to meet track supposedly being laid southward from Prince George. The tracks did not meet. Because of unbelievable physical difficulties encountered in building a long steel bridge over that river, and because of financial difficulties undergone in the post-war depression, work ceased. Original estimates had been exceeded, and they seemed enormous to a public which now doubted the necessity of further construction. Until 1925 the railroad became the subject of so many political investigations that the public wearied of its railway. People saw it being used as a "political football" and demanded the establishment of a new, non-political board of directors which would make the railway a paying proposition.

Not until gold was mined successfully at Bridge River and at Fred Wells's Cow Mountain did profits appear, and they did so because of the freight rates. With the coming of World War II, however, mining again declined and the railway faced further deficits. When in 1942 any steel which had been laid north of Quesnel was pulled and sent to Vancouver as war material, Quesnel feared that once and for all, after thirty years of hoping, plans for the original railroad had been finally shelved. The reverse was actually the truth.

During the war Cariboo lumbering developed and the interior of the province took on an appearance of permanency that had not hitherto existed. In June of 1945 Premier John Hart announced that the Pacific Great Eastern was to be projected to Dawson Creek by way of Pine Pass. The province then would have access to a 2,700,000-ton coal field, would develop the northern areas, and would have a part in Canada's growing defense plans. The following year survey parties staked the line which steel was to follow, and in July 1949 construction of the railway began once more. The survey now crosses the Cottonwood River seven miles above the original crossing.

The Pacific Great Eastern Railway had been good for Quesnel. During the construction period river boats carried freight for both the Pacific Great Eastern and Grand Trunk Pacific. The people saw John A. Fraser, their choice for the Legislature, reveal his fighting nature. The company planned to situate the station far from town because construction through the village would be too expensive, but Fraser felt that an out-of-town location would mean the beginning of a new and rival community, and after many meetings, interviews and speeches, had the station built where it stands today. With buildings erected to house equipment, the railway had a vested interest in the settlement and was therefore more willing to assist town development. This willingness is evident in the village's ability to lease Pacific Great Eastern land on which to build power plants. By railway, heavy equipment may be carried into an area fairly reasonably and heavy equipment is required for quartz mining. The coming of the railroad was, therefore, the signal for quartz prospectors to take to the hills. After 1945 lumber operations flourished because transportation was available to ship peeler logs, pit-props, telephone poles and pulpwood lengths to the coast. New people did move into the area, and the town doubled its population in a few years (though the farming communities remained small because most of the newcomers stayed right in town), but the anticipated influx of colonists never did come to Cariboo. Life on a small farm is too difficult, prices are too high, and markets too sparse.

Eventually, Cariboo's railway was extended to Vancouver from Squamish, and to the north. The Pacific Great Eastern reached Prince George on October 31, 1952 and reached Dawson Creek in October 1958. Cariboo finally had the line promised in election after election since 1912.

CHAPTER SIXTEEN

Links of Communication

The Cariboo Road is the key to the Cariboo. When this road opened, the Quesnel Forks trail to the mines was abandoned except by foot travellers. Occasional packers with small outfits of seven to ten animals, each of which would carry hundred-pound sacks of gold, also used the Quesnel Forks trail to meet the express at the Mountain House. For years the townspeople of Quesnel have advocated the opening of a good road from the mouth to the forks of the Quesnel River for access to the agricultural lands and gold areas of Likely and Horsefly. In 1952 the demand was still great, with the added reason that the Quesnel River is too rough for booming logs and a road would give southeast loggers access to rail head. But proponents of an access road over the years, including the *Cariboo Observer*, have had no more success than did Captain Mitchell, who had first advocated one in 1860.

Quesnel has always been bridge conscious as well as road conscious because the town is almost wrapped in a curve at the confluence of two rivers. When the road was constructed in 1865, no bridge was built and by 1873 the people, who were still using a rope ferry after eight years, were demanding one. In 1875 D. F. Adams obtained the contract and bridged the Quesnel; the bridge was washed out that same year but was rebuilt. While it was out, James Carson operated a ferry. He made $100 a day, but, being a prospector, kept little.

No bridge crossed the Fraser until 1929. In order to cross the murky river before 1910, one drifted down and across in a canoe, generally embarking near the telegraph office and landing across from the steamer wharf. Horses and cattle were forced to swim the terrible current and many were lost. F. E. Fairey tells of seeing a half-broken horse packed with a man's worldly goods being pushed into the river, carried by the current, sinking, coming up, climbing out at Red Bluff, and bucking his way out of sight. In December 1910 a cable for a ferry was hung across old Tacoutche Tesse, and the first to cross it were Capt. D. A. Foster, Harry Joyce and "Red" Unland. In 1927 the Quesnel River bridge, the longest wooden span in the province, was razed even though many people cried that the old bridge was in good condition and should not have been torn down. They probably thought they would not get another one, but they did, and immediately raised a cry for a bridge across the Fraser. Finally built, the Fraser River Bridge opened in March 1929.

Mail too was always a problem in the area. Originally the post was packed over the road to Cariboo by men like Barnard, but later the government arranged to have it transported to central depots. Until 1864 the mail distribution centre was at Williams Lake, but in 1863 Williams Lake was even by-passed by the road, whereas Quesnel was served by steamers and was a growing centre of population. In 1864 the office was withdrawn from the southern district and several other offices were established in the more immediate mining area where men could call for their mail or from where lists showing names of people for whom mail was waiting could be carried to the creeks by the miners. The Soda Creek and Van Winkle offices were established at this time, as were those at Williams Creek and Quesnellemouth. The Williams Creek office, the eighth in the province, was first operated by J. R. Commeline and later by John Bowron.

The post office at Quesnellemouth, under the direction of J. B. Gaggin, was located on Front Street near the Hudson's Bay corner, and from 1865 until 1911 it also served as telegraph office. In 1871 Abraham Barlow was both telegraph operator and line repair man on a salary of $30 a month. When in that year the postal service became a Federal government responsibility, Barlow became postmaster as well as telegrapher. On July 1, 1872 the name of the office was changed to Quesnelle. Ten years later when Barlow became a trader his daughter, Miss Isabel Barlow, replaced him in both jobs. Postal rates, even at that late date, were high. A letter from Quesnelle to Victoria cost 25¢ and to intermediate points, 12½¢; nevertheless, this was a great decrease from the $2 charged by Barnard in 1859. In 1900 the name of the settlement finally became known as Quesnel. In 1911 a new telegraph office was built on the bank of the river, and C. H. Allison, the town's first real druggist, had the post office in an extension to his store. When the drug store was sold in 1949, a post office building was rented until the present Federal Building opened in November 1953.

Other post offices appeared in the area as needed. The Van Winkle office was withdrawn before Confederation, but re-opened on July 1, 1872 with J. L. Linhard as post master. The Soda Creek office continued, but in July 1872 was operated by Robert McLeese and was located in his hotel. At Keithley in 1877 G. A. Veith was postmaster. The office at Quesnel Forks closed in 1923, but new ones at Australian and Cinema opened with E. Gray at the former and Miss E. M. Freto at the latter.

In 1911, when the telegraph office and post office separated, a new telegraph office building was erected also on the bank of the Fraser. This service operated without further improvement until 1926 when the Dominion government established telephone communication with Prince George. Louis LeBourdais, the telegraph operator at the time, was the first person to speak over this system. Six years later direct telephone connections were established with Vancouver and other points served by the British Columbia Telephone Company when the Dominion government system was linked with the radio-telephone service of the North West Telephone Co. By 1936 most stations on the old Yukon line from Hazelton north were served by short wave radio.

Because population was concentrating at Quesnel, the town gradually became the centre of the system. The only large group of people elsewhere was at Wells, and the Barkerville telegraph connection was moved to Wells in 1939. The flaw in this federal government communiction system was that all calls south, to Ashcroft for instance, had to pass through a relay system at the 150 Mile House, and when this flaw was overcome in 1939, after seventy-three years, the 150 Mile House lost its importance as a communication junction. The Dominion Telegraphs, owned by the Federal government, purchased the Quesnel Telephone Company in 1948, and on April 1, 1954 the British Columbia Telephone and Northwest Telephone took over the Canadian government telephone, but not telegraph, service.

In 1912 some of the more progressive members of the community had formed the Quesnel Telephone Company Limited, the original subscribers being E. L. Kepner, C. H. Allison, A. M. Farquhar, and E. J. Avison. A limited liability company with an authorized capital of $50,000 divided into 50,000 shares of one dollar each, the company was incorporated on December 31, 1912 with Kepner and Allison as directors; the object of the company was to supply the necessary public utilities in the town. The following year Avison was made a director, and the secretary, A. S. Vaughan, was allotted fifty shares. This group carried on until January 7, 1926 when Allison and Avison resigned and Fred D. and Ida May Abbott were appointed to the directorship. The last local director was Hyacinthe Mary Grierson who ceased to hold office in March 1936. Direction then came from the Pacific Power and Water Company Limited in Vancouver. In April 1949 the company filed its last annual report.

Quesnel's history has been made generally through road, steamer and rail communication, as well as telegraph services, but on October 23, 1928, the first aircraft landed on Dragon Lake. Four years later, R. L. "Ginger" Coote laid out a flying field on Baker Creek, on the west side of the Fraser. He planned a new passenger and airmail service in 1938, but instead joined the Royal Flying Corps. A more suitable landing field was selected in 1945, and a radio beam erected on Red Bluff. With fourteen-passenger Lodestars, Canadian Pacific Airlines inaugurated their first flights in 1946, making it possible to reach Quesnel from Vancouver in three hours. It had taken twenty hours by automobile, and more than three times that by stage coach.

The first radio was brought into town by C. H. Allison in 1923, but in the matter of communication one of the most important steps was the establishing of a radio station by Fred Weber, James Ritchie and Dennis Reid. CKCQ, operating at 1000 watts on 570 kilocycles, broadcast first on September 14, 1957. Heard as far north as Topley Landing in the Babine area, the station helps unify the entire Cariboo district by an interchange of information and a general philosophy of service. The owners chose Quesnel for the location of their $70,000 station because they felt that Quesnel was, is and always will be the centre of the Cariboo.

CHAPTER SEVENTEEN

Early Industries

Historically speaking, five industries developed the Quesnel area. On transportation, itself an industry, the other four—fur trading, mining, agriculture and lumbering—depend and these four industries are themselves related in certain ways. Other industries of lesser importance appeared, but in time faded away. By September 1865, for instance, Kerr and Duhig advertised their "Columbia Pale Ale and Porter" from Quesnellemouth Brewery. Kerr was the brewer and the quality was "unsurpassed," but the partnership dissolved and Duhig became the proprietor of a hotel. No other brewery operated, although in 1910, J. A. Fraser and W. L. Collins organized the Northern Interior Brewing Company, and George Breuder was to be their brewmaster. In May 1912 Hilborn and Smith began the Quesnel Brick Company on the bank of the Quesnel River but failed because there was no demand for the product. Machine shops, blacksmiths and lesser local works might perhaps be called "industries," but they added little to the town.

Fur traders open a country but discourage colonization; settlement both drives the animals farther away and brings a certain change in the Indians, making them more interested in settlement than in going to the wilderness for fur. Mining, on the other hand, brings settlement. Seldom does a miner intend staying in a vicinity to which he goes for gold, but circumstances often force him to establish himself permanently near the gold fields. These men become traders and farmers in order to supply other miners. Agriculture grows directly from the needs of the miners who must be fed, and usually local crops are cheaper than those that have to be imported. Hence early farmers in the area were successful. As farmers and traders group themselves together, and as the villages grow, the log house becomes too cumbersome, too unsightly; finished lumber is desired for interiors. In this way the lumber industry starts. This pattern was followed in the Quesnel area.

After Mackenzie saw the new area, after Stuart had started trading, after Fraser had made his trip to the sea, the North West Company began to develop the fur trade of New Caledonia. The Company shipped about eighty bales of fur, mostly mink, marten and beaver, to Fort Chipewyan and later to Fort Kamloops. Although this was no great amount the Hudson's Bay Company made plans as early as 1819 to invade the beaver trade of the area, but the amalgamation of the companies in 1821 eliminated any rivalry. The fort at Alexandria was not at first to be used by the Hudson's Bay Company, as the new commercial grouping was called, but was opened in September 1821 when the brigade trail to Kamloops came into use and trade went through Pacific ports.

Life at a Hudson's Bay fort in New Caledonia was not easy, although only about one fifth of an employee's time was spent working. Company profits came from hardships necessarily inflicted on the men, but anyone at a post with a position of "Clerk," or higher, shared in the profits. A Clerk in charge of a station of some importance might receive a salary of $500 a year. The next highest position was Chief Trader; together, a Clerk and Chief Trader at a station were known as "wintering partners." The Postmaster, although well qualified as interpreter and trader, was not ranked so high as Clerk, although he may have been in charge of a post. Ranked between postmaster and common labourers in more or less militiary gradations were interpreters, guides, mechanics, steersmen, canoe bowmen, middlemen, and others.

There was hustle and bustle when the Indians were near, but after they had gone to winter quarters to obtain furs, life at the post was dreary. In 1833 a travelling subscription library was started, but lasted only ten years. Many of the men were well educated and ardent readers; others played the violin or flute; some wrote magnificent letters. Nevertheless, the sameness became trying and only rare visits from officials broke the monotony.

The food was dreary, too: a steady diet of dried salmon, and not always enough of that. Fort McLeod men hauled salmon 106 miles from Stuart Lake by dog sled. A year's supply of fish on hand, both for food and trading purposes, was deemed necessary. The company bought salmon from the Indians at the rate of one beaver skin to ninety salmon, and later in the year, when the Indians were often in need of food, the company sold or exchanged dried fish for pelts, thereby making another profit. In 1836 at Fort Fraser alone the company required 36,000 salmon.

Meat of a young bear was a welcome change or, if nothing else, "giddee" or Indian dog was variety for the menu. Dried salmon and fifty pounds of flour per man were provided by the company, and employees sought other food locally with gun, fish-hook or net, but they had no salt. The area was known as the "Botany Bay" of the fur trade.

Traders remained at the forts, and Indians went to the wilds in the fall after having spent the summer encamped around the company quarters. All summer the company extended credit to the Indians to insure their returning to the bush. If the native came back in the spring without pelts, he received no further credit. For a gun bought in the summer, the Indian contracted to bring six beaver skins to the fort the following spring; for a "two point" blanket, four skins; for a "three point" blanket, six skins. The skin, as a unit of value, was presumed to weigh one pound and was called, technically, a "Made Beaver," or "M.B." Merchandise was priced in "M.B.'s" or fractions thereof. Peter Skene Ogden, Chief Factor in charge of New Caledonia from 1835 to 1844, tried to curb the credit system, but managed only to reduce the loans of guns, axes, traps and moose skins, because Indians invariably had plausible excuses for not returning them.

Despite its size the establishment of New Caledonia was not exceptionally profitable. Moose skins had to be imported from Fort Chipewyan to make shoes and leather: the sinews were used for thread; the parchment skin, for horses' nose bags and for window panes. The number of men required was almost twice that needed in other areas of the same size. The company, too, required many kinds of furs, but reaped no great variety from New Caledonia. The years from 1843 to 1846 were dismally poor ones and the company only made a profit by paying a tenth of what it paid for furs on the coast.

Regardless of the amount of fur collected the catch had to go to Fort Vancouver from Fort St. James. As the brigades gathered, forts took on new life: clerks bargained for the catch while assistants tagged and bundled it into bales of about one hundred pounds. Leaving Stuart Lake toward the end of May, a flotilla of batteaux, "North Canoes," would move down the Stuart River. These boats were of whaleboat design, clinker-built, but smaller than those of the east: 40 to 50 feet long, 6 feet amidships, of birchbark sewn together with spruce fibres and daubed with pine resin. A flooring of pine board in each prevented breakage. They were pointed at both ends and had no keel. Each carried six men, two of whom were veterans of the trip: one of the veterans steered, the other sat in front; four middlemen paddled. The canoes carried forty bales of fur, five hundred pounds of provisions and each man's forty pounds of personal luggage, a total of about five thousand pounds.

People remaining at the post cheered the gaily decked, happy group with the Chief Factor in the leading canoe, as the flotilla started down stream. At Fort Fraser it was joined by more batteaux. At Fort George, two days later, canoes were checked, letters written, dispatches received and more voyageurs from the north and east assembled. From there, the company passed like corks down the river, through Cottonwood Canyon, past the Quesnel, to Fort Alexandria.

Fort Alexandria was the great trans-shipment centre, "Stella-yeh," the end of navigation, and held the same position in fur-trading days that Quesnel held during the gold rush. The post itself did collect thirty to forty bales of peltries a year, taken from the eastern side of the river, and received four bales from Fort Chilcotin, but Alexandria's great importance was as a loading centre, and all the facilities for such a centre were concentrated there. At this point, goods were unloaded from the boats and packed onto sleek, fat pack-horses to be taken 215 miles to Fort Kamloops and on to Fort Okanogan, a trip of twenty days. While the pack-horses—from forty to four hundred in number—wound their way south, led by the Factor who was preceded by scouts, people at Fort Alexandria repaired the boats for the return journey. On his return to Alexandria the Factor carried necessary supplies for the northern posts and there directed the transfer of the supplies from pack animals to boats. In another twenty days they were back at Stuart Lake.

The Hudson's Bay Company naturally feared and resented the coming of miners for several reasons. During the excitement of gold fever men often left the company to mine or, knowing the value of trade, to retail supplies. Miners, too, eventually retired, some, like Peter Curran Dunlevy, to become opposition. The Company then resorted to any means to drive away competition. Sometimes it failed, but generally, as the more powerful organization, it won. At times, in order to lure Indian trade to the posts, the Company resorted to selling liquor to the Indians. Competition, too, was often the forerunner of colonization and with colonization fur bearing animals retreated farther into the hills, sometimes beyond the reach of the natives.

Although gold had been found on the mainland, James Douglas withheld news of the discovery from the public for as long a time as possible in order to keep his company together. This attitude towards miners was responsible for the slowness of the early rush and was not changed until Peter Dunlevy managed to purchase supplies at Fort Kamloops. From that time the Company realized that a fortune was to be made in supplying goods directly to newcomers. The miners came and the fur trade was ruined.

With the opening of the Quesnel store in September 1866, business increased somewhat. Many farmers trapped on their lands and miners trapped during the winter to eke out a living. Catches were sold to the Hudson's Bay Company at Quesnel or, after June 1867, at Barkerville. Free fur traders like Elmore, Davis, or Robert Armstrong, wandered about the country. The brigade trails deteriorated when the Company began shipping bales by boat to Soda Creek and by wagon to the south over the new road. Business slackened because the Indians, preferring to serve the white man otherwise than as trapper, took manual labour in the settled areas. The Indians' desire for farm horses provided the Company with a partial solution to its problems. It reduced the price of furs and the reduction forced the Indian to trap longer; he required more furs in order to purchase a horse. To be doubly sure, the Company then raised the selling price of goods, a manoeuvre which held the fur trade at a level of some importance. In 1872, however, when Peter

Toy and "Twelve Foot" Davis descended from Peace River with excellent marten pelts, the company faced an influx of free traders. Davis promised Hugh Gillis of Quesnel 2,000 prime beaver pelts the following year. In the London market beaver sales almost collapsed when changing styles in headgear wrought the destruction of the trade, though independent traders continued to operate. At Quesnel in 1884, Telesphore Marion purchased furs which he shipped directly to England and which, therefore, never came into the hands of the Company.

Today, the fur industry has all but disappeared. Although some trapping is done, all furs are sent to agents in Vancouver. In 1945 the British Columbia Registered Trappers' Association attempted to further the industry and to protect all game through its connection with the *Cariboo Digest.*

The coming of the miners did more than disrupt the fur trade, for the Cariboo district of British Columbia, one of the world's richest gold fields, may perhaps be the birthplace of British Columbia. In attracting a population from the world over, Cariboo indirectly brought the formation of a Crown Colony and eventually, a confederation of the colony with Canada.

Gold mining in Cariboo depends on the price of gold as well as on the price of goods and labour. Producing mines often closed because of the costs of transporting machinery and goods, and because of increased operating expenses on the labour front. The Cariboo is not a great gold producer today, but as in days of old, away from the busy centre of Wells, one may see an ancient Chinese at a sluice box or with a washing pan, and old prospectors continue their search for the mother lode. Although the Second Cariboo Gold Rush is finished, experts will not predict when a third will commence.

Production by placer in British Columbia from 1858 to 1949 is estimated at $93,093,524. Platinum, rather than gold, accounted for $93,137 between 1887 and 1945. Most production came from the Cariboo gold fields, an area of about 7,000 square miles which forms the watershed of the Horsefly, Quesnel, Cottonwood and Willow rivers. Of them all, Williams Creek has produced the most.

In 1861 Williams Creek was discovered by "Dutch Bill" Dietz

when he crossed Bald Mountain from the diggings on Antler Creek. Williams Creek carried three paystreaks: one at the surface and two below; of the three, the last two were the richest, but required more capital to work. In the early years the amounts taken from various claims by panning, rocking and sluicing were fabulous. On some days Steel's claim gave over 400 ounces; $100,000 was taken from this 80-by-25-foot claim. During the season of 1862 William Cunningham's claim yielded $2,000 a day. In shallow ground of 30 feet, these claims were above the canyon. In 1861 William Barker sank a shaft below the canyon and Diller followed his example. It is said that gold worth $38,400 was taken from Diller's shaft, 50 to 70 feet deep. The section of creek below the canyon, from the Black Jack to Mason Meadows, produced between nine and twelve millions of dollars; the upper part produced about eight millions.

Gold was panned, sluiced or rockered all week and in most cases seven days a week. Diller boasted that he would never leave his diggings until he could take out his own weight, 240 pounds, in gold. He did better, for when he had the 240 pounds, he weighed out enough to balance his 120-pound dog. Except for H. F. "Twelve Foot" Davis's claim, only one on the creek from Marysville to San Juan gave less than $25,000; that one, $10,000. The Cameron claim was almost the top producer with $800,000. Only the Aurora, with $850,000, had more. Williams Creek alone accounted for nearly seventeen and a half million dollars and the tributary gulches, Eureka, McArthur's, Walker's, Conklin's and McCallum's account for approximately two million. The total is over nineteen million dollars. These figures cannot be taken as complete by any means, because gold left the district without being reported. Later production added millions more because some claims were productive for another fifty years.

Williams Creek, with those main tributaries, was the most valuable of the Cariboo strikes: a tough place to live, a tough place to work; a place where money came easily, but where prices were high. If one could leave with a sizeable amount he would find cheap living at the coast in those days of generally low prices. Thousands of people scrambled for the gold. In 1862, 727 claims were staked on this creek; the following year, 1863, 3,071. Labourers were paid $10 a day; room and board cost $35 a week. Food costs were high and new work trousers cost $20. Probably more than one miner dressed as did Jake Walker, of Walker's Gulch, in "discarded flour sacks sewn together with the remains of the various brands that had once advertised the contents of the sacks appearing in all directions on the surface." Byron Johnson, the man who met Walker and noted his garb, also described the creek as it was in 1863:

> For two or three miles down Williams Creek all the available ground appeared to be taken up, and the place bore a wonderful resemblance to an ant's nest. The unfortunate little stream had been treated in the most ignominious manner. A little above the town [Barkerville] it flowed along silvery and clear as it had been wont to do; but soon inroads were made upon its volume in the shape of ditches cut from it, and continued along the sides of the hills, to feed the huge over-shot water-wheels that appeared in all directions. Then its course became diverted into five or six different channels, which were varied every now and then as the miners sought to work the surface formerly covered by them. At intervals dirty streams were poured forth by the sluices, in which the earth dug from beneath was being washed by the water; and here and there the stream was insulted by being shut up for a few hundred yards in a huge wooden trough, called a "flume."
>
> Across the breadth of the little valley was a strange heterogeneous gathering of smaller flumes, carrying water to the different diggings and supported at various heights from the ground by props, windlasses at the mouths of shafts, water-wheels, banks of 'tailings' (the refuse earth washed through the sluices), and miners' log huts.
>
> On the sides of the hills the primeval forests had been cleared for a short distance upwards, to provide timber for mining purposes, and logs for the huts. These abodes were more numerous on the hill sides than in the bottom of the valley, as being more safe from removal.
>
> The town comprised the ordinary series of rough wooden shanties, stores, restaurants, grog shops, and gambling saloons; and, on a little eminence, the official residence, tenanted by the Gold Commissioner and his assistants and one policeman, with the British flag permanently displayed in front of it, looked over the whole.
>
> In and out of this nest the human ants poured all day and night, for in wet-sinking the labour must be kept up without ceasing all through the twenty-four hours, Sundays included. It was a curious sight to look down the creek at night, and see each shaft with its little fire, and its lantern, and the dim ghostly figures gliding about from darkness to light, like the demons at a Drury Lane pantomime, while an occasional hut was illuminated by some weary labourer returning from his nightly toil.

The word here seemed to be WORK, and nothing else; only round the bar-rooms and gambling tables were a few loafers and gamblers to be seen. Idling was too expensive a luxury in a place where wages were from two to three pounds per day, and flour sold at six shillings a pound.

The mingling of noises was as curious as that of objects. From the hills came the perpetual crackling and thudding of axes, intermingling with the crash of falling trees, and the grating undertone of the saws, as they fashioned the logs into planks and boards. From the bottom of the valley rose the splashing and creaking of waterwheels, the grating of shovels, the din of the blacksmith's hammer sharpening pickaxes, and the shouts passed from the tops of numerous shafts to the men below, as the emptied bucket was returned by the windlass.

Williams Creek itself eclipsed all others for colour, rowdiness gaiety and production. Along with its tributary gulches and creeks, the area continued to pay for many years. The Black Jack operated until 1890 and the Black Jack Hydraulic took out $10,000 in 1897. One of the last activities, a five-man Barkerville company, hydraulicked the El Dorado, next to Black Jack, with water from Williams Creek and Conklin's gulch in two miles of ditch and 650 feet of 7-inch pipe. The gold was coarse and had much quartz attached. Gold at that time was worth only $15.95 an ounce, and the costly operations only paid expenses. Cariboo Gold Fields Limited held miles of Williams Creek, but after spending a million dollars and after many costly failures, took a total of $36,000 in 1902 and 1903 from ground previously worked by old timers whose timbers and sets still stand on the channel. Lane and Kurtz's Cariboo Gold Mining Company worked another four miles along the creek, but slum and the inrush of water forced them to abandon their scheme.

Stout's Gulch, discovered in 1861 by Edward Stout who had been with Dietz in discovering Williams Creek, is part of an ancient stream. The Alturis claim there, which sold for $23,000 and repaid that amount in five weeks, produced $275,000; the Taafe Vale, $300,000; the Wintrip, which worked for twenty-five years, $250,000. John Hopp hydraulicked for years and worked to the summit, to where the gulch connects with Lowhee Creek. This entire gulch was a network of timbers, the remains of which may be seen today. Although great labour is required, pay-ground may still be worked.

At the confluence of Walker's Gulch and the Williams Creek channel, two miles above Stout's Gulch, stands the Richfield courthouse and the remains of the rooms in which Judge Begbie lived while in residence. This gulch, worked until 1922, has produced $100,000. Forest Rose Gulch, at the Mason Meadows end of the rich area, was being worked as late at 1912, hydraulic equipment having been installed in 1876. Conklin's Gulch, on the east side of the creek, produced a million and a half dollars with the chief claims being the Aurora, the Sawmill and the Ericson.

Other creeks were of great importance, not the least being Antler where the same "babel of busy mortals" toiled for gold. The production of Antler and its tributaries is estimated at six million dollars, but is really unknown. Only logs remain at the site of McAlinen's store and saloon of the old town, but the names of the old claims continue to give a lift to the adventurous. One still hears talk of Nason, Lothair, and China Creek, or one may still shovel a pan of dirt to swirl in the now-muddy Antler or Pleasant creeks. The Waverly Mine began there in 1868 and worked for fifty years.

The Willow River drainage system includes Lowhee Creek from which Richard Willoughby and his partners took $140,000 and then sold for a high price. About two miles long, the creek had been worked within a mile of the apex at Stout's Gulch. After being thoroughly worked by early prospectors, it was hydraulicked for twenty years to produce between four and five million dollars. Cariboo Consolidated Limited acquired the rights on Lowhee Creek and, in 1907, John Hopp worked it with water from Jack of Clubs Lake.

Lightning Creek was the great rival of Williams Creek, but did not last so long. Its total production is estimated at eight millions. The problem there was water pressure. During the first years of the rush, Captain Evans and the Welsh party sank a shaft, but water defeated them. Two other outfits drove a drainage tunnel 3,000 feet, but met slum and lost their timbers. Nevertheless, this area was worked by F. J. Tregillus, Harry Jones and J. Price at the turn of the century; as late as 1918, a thousand ounces were taken from Perkin's Gulch. The slum problem persists.

At Wingdam, in 1878, the Big Bonanza Company sank a shaft,

but was driven out by water. Two years later a New York company spent a million and a half on buildings and equipment, but though some of the buildings, the shaft houses and the machinery remain, mining operations have ceased. As late as 1946 the problem of the great flow of underground water had not been overcome.

At the mouth of the Cottonwood, where it joins the Fraser, banks of cemented auriferous gravels contain gold, but to release the gold from the cement is too costly. At one time hopes were high that hydraulic would be effective if the gravels were broken down and allowed to weather for a year. This failed. A mill was then tried, but that too failed. The latest decision was that hydraulic under a very high head would be effective.

Hixon Creek, a tributary of the Fraser and worked in 1866, produced coarse gold for a distance of two and a half miles. The creek had never been properly bottomed, and E. Edens of Stanley sank a shaft 90 feet only to hit slum. In 1890 the Blue Lead Hydraulic Company constructed a ditch, hauled in pipe and a monitor with a view to undertaking hydraulic operations, but expenses proved too high. Small operators cannot afford continuous operations and the project always fails.

The Quesnel River watershed, the largest drainage basin of Cariboo, was the earliest to be discovered, but was not on a main thoroughfare until the road to that district was constructed through Williams Lake; the Beaver Lake, Keithley and Horsefly areas came more under the domination of Williams Lake than of Quesnel. The total gold production from this area between 1874 and 1945 has been estimated at 288,167 ounces or $5,435,915. Cunningham Creek was discovered in 1861 and William Cunningham took 600 ounces of coarse gold from a crevice on the west branch, but the creek was not actively worked until three years later when there was a rush back from Williams Creek. Cunningham Creek was then panned profitably by Chinese and was hydraulicked for years afterwards as a paying proposition. Keithley was the fourth richest creek in early Cariboo, surpassed only by Williams, Lightning and Antler, and parts of Keithley Creek have been mined as many as six times, paying returns on each working. Other great streams of world-wide interest were Spanish, producing $77,349 and Cedar Creek, with $654,227. "Aurora Jack" of Conklin's Gulch lost money at Cedar Creek when the Aurora there did not produce more than $30,000, which did not pay expenses. Cedar Creek was rediscovered in 1921.

One of the greatest placer undertakings was Joseph Hunter's damming of the Quesnel Lake outlet in order to clean up gold in the south fork channel. At a cost of $500,000 he built the dam in 1897 and 1898 with 500 men. The company, an English family, operated for a year at a cost of $76,000 and took out nearly $223,000. Quesnel Forks is now abandoned and bears no resemblance to the days when it was the great centre of Cariboo, although for years a Chinese family operated a store in the shadow of the hills. The scars of the forest fire which burned so fiercely in 1869 and which killed so many Chinese between the Forks and Twenty Mile Creek are still apparent. Between 1874 and 1945 this part of the river produced 120,187 ounces of gold, 48,884 of them between 1896 and 1900.

Of all the mines developing between the first and second Cariboo Gold rushes, the Bullion, on Dancing Bill's Gulch, was perhaps the most spectacular and was considered to be the greatest hydraulic enterprise in the world. The Chinese had done well on Dancing Bill's for many years. In 1892 the Canadian Pacific Railway acquired the rights and organized the Cariboo Hydraulic Mining Company with a capital of $2,500,000. In ten years, the operation produced over a million dollars, but was totally dependent on the fluctuations of water. In 1900, the biggest year, there were rumours that an attempt would be made to rob the stage carrying the gold. It is said that J. B. Hobson, the manager, had the gold cast in one cylindrical block weighing 145 pounds troy: if the stage were stopped bandits would find it impossible to carry away the huge brick. It was exhibited in Toronto and went eventually to the United States Mint.

The present town of Quesnel was also an early producer. Ben MacDonald first turned the yellow sand at the mouth of the Quesnel River, and shortly afterwards Ferguson's or Rich Bar returned three ounces a day per man. Long Bar, seven miles up-river, also produced for many years. Campan, or Gravel Creek, which was worked by Chinese, produced a reputed $1,250,000. Opposite the mouth of the Quesnel River is an old channel, the edge of which is cut by Baker Creek. C. F. Law of Vancouver sank a shaft 300 feet in the channel and although he found gold all the way down, he found none on bedrock. Later investigators decided that he had not really hit bedrock, but merely superimposed strata.

The production of gold in Cariboo was extremely high from the first discovery until the Second Gold Rush in the 1930s. The dollar total taken from the Quesnel River watershed is approximately twenty-seven millions; from Williams Creek and its tributaries, twenty-six millions; Antler, six millions; Willow, eight millions; Lightning, eight millions. An estimated four millions have possibly not been counted, having been shipped or carried out before adequate means of control were instituted,; and the Chinese, whose custom was to send money home to China, may be assumed to have exported some. About one million came from the Fraser River at Quesnel. Between 1874 and 1945, when mining may be presumed to have ended, the Cariboo Mining Division produced 539,572 ounces of gold worth $10,936,626.

After the shallow diggings were finished—after the areas had been panned, sluiced or rockered by the original argonauts—further development in placer mining required huge capital outlay. Hydraulic works are expensive to install, shafts costly to sink, and stamp mill costs exorbitant for small operators. The Quesnel Lake Dam and the Bullion are illustrative of the capital required to develop mines after 1865. The prospector with his pan and the little group with a rocker but without money were forced to new districts where the possibilities of early successes were greater. As early as 1862 Rock Creek beckoned to many who felt this happening on Williams Creek. Later Big Bend, Peace River, Cassiar, Yukon attracted attention. By 1923 only those who may have made strikes several times in the past remained, but they had usually poured their money back into the ground and were again hoping to find the great pocket, the Mother Lode. These men who continued prospecting, and who continued adding to the amounts of gold from Cariboo, eventually becoming interested in quartz mining and were responsible for the new gold rush of the 1930s when British Columbia was in desperate need of new discoveries. The years 1927 to 1930 had accounted for the lowest gold returns since 1858.

Placer mining had one last enthusiastic period when the dragline dredge came into its own. By 1938 E. G. Degalia of San Francisco prepared to dredge ten miles along the meadows of old Williams

Creek. Early in 1914 the Yukon Gold Mining Company Limited had dredged both Antler and Williams creeks at a profit, the latter from Stout's Gulch to the Meadows. The Degalia group, nevertheless, did well. At the beginning of World War II, dredge work began at Moffat Flats near Alexandria and was successful even though the gold was exceedingly fine. In 1946 the first machine dredged the Quesnel River, and the North America Goldfields group was successful on Spanish Creek. Fishing interests opposed dredge lines on the Quesnel for they feared that the muck would ruin the Quesnel Lake spawning grounds, but when this objection proved to be false more outfits came into the river. The California group, headed by F. Smith and D. Anderson, dredged the Cottonwood with success, and by using floodlights for night work E. A. Kent was able to work three shifts on the Swift. This type of expensive mining is limited to the streams alone. The future of Cariboo mining really depends on quartz, although in 1958 people were again talking "dredge."

Quartz had been scoffed at for years and the emphasis was on placer. Blair, Tregillus, Armstrong and Carey, however, continued prospecting but with an eye for quartz. Fred Wells was another who went from vein to vein panning samples, sinking tunnels, and drilling test holes. Not until 1932 did Cow Mountain Tunnel prove his methods to be right. Being as shrewd a promoter as he was a prospector, Wells formed the Cariboo Gold Quartz Company. Starting as a small mill crushing 50 tons of ore a day, by 1936, even after posting a dividend the year before, the mill enlarged to 275 tons capacity and produced about $700,000 a year. Across Jack of Clubs Lake from Cariboo Gold Quartz, the New York-owned Newport Mining Corporation's Island Mountain produced nearly $900,000 from November 1934 to April 1936.

The future of lode mining is questionable in view of present-day circumstances. During the war, practically no work was done and Wells became almost as ghost town. Just as the mines commenced working again, strikes threatened the industry. After 1947, however, the mine employed 250 men, milled 300 tons daily, and had hopes of a good steady future because of further discoveries. Island Mountain ceased operation in 1954, and though Cariboo Gold Quartz produced 41,464 ounces of gold and 3,989 ounces of silver in 1955, it too eventually closed.

Perhaps the lode mine most interesting to Quesnel has been in the Hixon Hills, for though this area between Prince George and Quesnel did not bring prosperity to the town, it was exploited by local people. A company created to mine the Hills purchased a five-stamp mill in 1879. James Reid was president and R. J. Skinner, who also managed the Hudson's Bay Company store, was secretary; W. A. Johnston had been a miner before becoming general road superintendent and later settling on Fernbrook Farm at the junction of the Fraser and Quesnel rivers; and Robert McLeese owned a store and hotel at Soda Creek, as well as the steamer *Victoria* which ran between Soda Creek and Quesnel. The company was frustrated by a shortage of money to meet rising freight rates, which were already high. In 1936 a new company, the Quesnelle Quartz Mining Company, invested in this region which had been idle since the original group ran out of money; the vice-president of the new company was Mrs. Charlotte Carey, formerly the wife of James Reid.

Gold, of course, is not the only mineral of Cariboo; there are others, both metallic and non-metallic, many of little importance at present: aluminum, arsenic, bismuth, chromium, copper, lead, iron, magnesium and manganese. Just prior to the depression a platinum extracting plant at Two Mile Flat had more success with gold than with platinum. On Hardscrabble Mountain a deposit of scheelite was first worked as placer in 1870: in 1937, a testing mill was introduced, but because of the distance from transportation there have been no great developments. The non-metallics include epsomite, carbonate and sulphate of soda, lime, mica, magnesite, leucite, barite, opal, talc, gypsum and silica. Once again because of transportation problems, the most interesting of these riches have not been greatly exploited.

Coal exists at Alexandria, Australian, and in the Bowron River area, but because it is of an inferior quality, it would be unprofitable to develop. Several attempts, other than local, have been made to use the coal, but without much success. E. A. Lee, R. Morgan and particularly Frank A. Patrick have tried to interest the public in Cariboo coal. The old steamer *Quesnel* burned local coal occasionally and in 1930 the Cariboo Coal and Clay Company supplied the Royal Bank in Quesnel with coal from Australian. World War II aroused more interest in the coal and in 1948 a better quality was found. Three years later F. H. Hutton of Vancouver planned to ship coal to the coast, but nothing has been done and probably nothing will be done until local industry requires local fuel. Oil is closely related to coal and various enthusiastic projects to drill wells have been suggested. Although a veritable rush to stake claims ensued in the early 1930s the hoped-for gushers never did materialize even though some drilling was still being done in 1953 and 1955.

The Quesnel area also contains a large reserve of diatomaceous earth which has been known since gold rush days. The diatomite looks like and feels like clay but is really almost pure calcium made from infinitesimal shells that were deposited millions of years ago. This material, it is said, has 750 uses, including insulation and water-proofing. Consolidated Mining and Smelting Company imports diatomite from California to use as an absorbing agent, and sugar refineries use the material as a filter. Beds of this earth extending thirty-five miles north and south of Quesnel on both sides of the river vary in depth from 2 to 50 feet, and every few years over the past century some one talks diatomite, but does nothing. In 1927 Canadian Diatomite looked it over; in 1929 the B.C. *Gazette* announced a diatomite factory for Quesnel; in 1946 a Calgary firm discussed shipping 3,000 tons annually for fertilizer. The Alberta Mud Company did ship four carloads but no more, partly because of the prohibitive freight costs.

By weight diatomite is 50% water, and because sun-drying the material has been unsatisfactory development will not progress until someone discovers a cheap, efficient method of removing the water. Hope was renewed in December 1954 when Westcoast Transmission announced that its natural gas pipeline would pass through Quesnel. On January 5, 1956 work began and on October 3, 1957 the company turned gas into the mains of the Inland Natural Gas Company at Quesnel. Before the end of that month rumours were flying that the answer to the problem of drying diatomite had been found. It had not.

The influx of miners brought the development of and the need for agriculture, but in a wide sense agriculture was first introduced to Cariboo long before the gold rush. Daniel Williams Harmon, one of the partners of the North West Company at Fort St. James, planted a garden in 1811. His journal for May of that year reports his activities: "As the frost is now out of the ground we have planted our potatoes and sowed barley, turnips, etc., which are the first that we ever sowed, on this west side of the mountain."

With evidence of good crops the company began growing its own grain, especially barley for horse feed, though processing some as cereal foods for servants of the company and more for green fodder. Between 1842 and 1848 the Hudson's Bay Company farm at Alexandria on Five Mile Flat east of the Fraser operated a portable flour mill. Of U.S. manufacture, with stones 2 feet in diameter, it had been bought at Fort Vancouver, taken up the Columbia by water to Fort Okanogan and from there by pack horse to this northern end of the brigade trail. The driving gear was build at Alexandria by a Canadian voyageur. By 1843 Alexandria was using 6,500 bushels of grain a year for flour. Alexander Douglas McInnes obtained these Hudson's Bay Company farmlands in 1880.

As miners moved into unlikely places, the adjacent lands possible to farm were pre-empted. By 1862 and 1862 Sumas and Chilliwack shipped farm products north, but at high prices, and it became imperative that necessities be grown close to hand, though most places did grow wheat, barley, oats, peas and potatoes. At the same time and for the same purpose, choice lands on the upper Fraser and close to the mining camps were taken for agricultural purposes.

On January 1, 1860 Governor Douglas promulgated the first pre-emption act, providing for the granting of rights to unsurveyed Crown lands— not more than 160 acres at a purchase price not exceeding ten shillings an acre. The fire which destroyed the town of Barkerville in 1868 also destroyed the government office with its official records, and the present records made afterwards from whatever material was available are, consequently, somewhat incomplete. Nevertheless, it is known that apart from settlement on Vancouver Island and the Lower Fraser Valley, Cariboo was one of the first areas to be farmed. In the register of Cariboo pre-emptions, the first entry, dated October 10, 1860, is a joint one for three parcels of land at Beaver Lake in the names of Richard Dorsey, Joseph and A. Deschields for 160 acres each. The land "in the valley of Beaver Lake about 28 miles E.N.E. of Alexandria" was the first of a series of farms which extended along the river, spread into various mining areas, and surrounded the area of the town of Quesnel. In fact, the town of Quesnel itself was pre-empted.

In truth, until recently, commercial agriculture in Cariboo has never been on a vast scale. Farmers who located along the Cariboo Road grew hay, oats, wheat and barley to be sold to the freighters as animal food. The great land holdings were most fortunate; because of their size, they grew large and varied crops. This was the agricultural picture for fifty years: food for horses and food for miners.

The outstanding early ranch was at Mud Lake, pre-empted in 1861 by G. Weaver and J. May, and later acquired by R. A. Collins for hay and pasturage. Collins also acquired the 1862 pre-emption of R. L. Brown and the 1868 recording of John Oscar Smith. In the same valley Robert McLeese, J. T. Lenay and Robert Stoddart recorded farms in 1863, though McLeese was the only one of the partners to obtain a Crown Grant for his property. At his death the land passed to his only daughter, Mrs. Jean Sinclair Foster, the wife of Capt. D. A. Foster of the Fraser River boat service. Born at Soda Creek she had been educated at Victoria and Tacoma, returning to Cariboo in 1902 where she had married.

By 1863 the Mud Lake, or McLeese Lake, settlement was expanding. Sellers and Hamilton and Company had a large log house, and Alexander Saunders, formerly an agent of the Hudson's Bay Company, had a store. Peter Curran Dunlevy, who was well established in a partnership at Beaver Lake, moved to Soda Creek when he realized that the new Cariboo Road would kill his Beaver Lake venture. In the new location, he started a hotel, saloon, store and ranch, but spent a fortune in trying to extract gold from Island Mountain ore. Dunlevy died at Soda Creek in 1904 and was buried at St. Joseph's Mission, Williams Lake.

The best known ranches immediately south of the Quesnel town are the Kersley and Australian. The latter is a community on the east bank of the Fraser River twenty-one miles south of Quesnel which derives its name from a group of pre-emptions located on October 6, 1863 by W. H. Downes, Stephen Downes and Andrew Olson. The original owners had come from Australia and named their ranch in honour of the Australian gold rush. Olson and his brother had pushed a unique trundle barrow up the Cariboo Road during the gold excitement. One of these one-wheeled barrows— just a set of handles in front for pulling, and a set of handles at the rear for pushing—was at the ranch for many years. These first settlers cleared the land without proper tools or animals at a time when a yoke of oxen cost $1,500 and a set of oak wheels from England cost the same. The present owners of the land purchased it in 1903. The Yorston Brothers, Robert and John, were originally stage drivers on the road, but acquired the ranch when they quit the staging business. John Yorston, who died in 1937, represented Cariboo for a number of years as a Liberal Member of the Legislative Assembly.

Adjoining the Australian, C. Mackenzie, Sam Brierly and A. Saunders located in 1861–62. These pre-emptions along with four other early ones, including the one Charles Kersley pre-empted on August 19, 1897, were purchased by Samuel Bohanon, but the Bohanon ranch has always been known as Kersley. Bohanon sold several lots and eventually all his interests in order to spend his declining years in Quesnel, where he died in 1927. The various holdings have been subdivided and sold as smaller blocks which permit mixed farming. The original Kersley House burned in February 1955.

In many places close to the mining areas, people pre-empted land and when the roads developed built stopping houses. At the mouth of Beaver Pass, at Lightning Creek, H. Georgeson and G. Buchanan pre-empted 160 acres in 1862. In 1872 George Hyde became the third owner of the land with which he also acquired the Beaver Pass stopping house. E. F. Edwards and his brother, W. "Bloody" Edwards, took land at Pine Grove Creek and conducted a stopping house. Dudley C. Moreland, J. C. Wade and G. M. Cox settled at the junction of Lightning Creek and the Swift River in 1862. The following year John Ryder established Cottonwood Farm, but sold to John Boyd in 1876 and moved closer to Quesnel town.

In the immediate vicinity of Quesnel, on June 8, 1861, Charles Danielson pre-empted "a triangular plot of land at the junction of the Quesnel and Fraser Rivers, bounded on the north by the Quesnel River and on the west by the Fraser." After living on the land for a year, he had "a house...on it and land cultivated and fenced." This was Fernbrook Farm, later owned by Alvin Johnston.

In certain regions, poor soil or poor climate discouraged cultivation. At Quesnel Forks the first gardener had packed seeds from the coast, planted them, and waited. Nothing ripened but radishes.

In the very early days a serious outbreak of scurvy occurred in the mining camps on Williams Creek, and miners coming out in the fall were anxious to obtain any kind of vegetable. Danielson had planted a patch of turnips which were ready at that time and he sold them at 25 cents to $1 each, making a profit of $3,000. With his profit he built a new ferry across the Quesnel River and refurbished the stopping house which he operated on the south bank. Thaddeus Harper then secured title for this lot and, with his brother Jerome, pastured cattle there. Originally from Virginia, the Harper brothers imported cattle from Oregon to Barkerville, grazed them on the mountains, and slaughtered twenty at a time as required. (The Harpers eventually required ranchland and bought what became the Gang Ranch on the Fraser, what became the Perry Ranch at Cache Creek, and what they called Harper's Camp east of Kamloops.) The lot next to this, "situated on the left bank of the Quesnel River about 1 mile from its mouth, extending ½ mile up river," J. Gilbert took on June 26, 1863 and transferred his rights the following year to Kwong Lee and Company, but in 1885 this company went bankrupt and the courts ordered the lot sold to Alfred Carson.

On August 17, 1863 three Frenchmen—Fabien Picard, Fabien *dit* Lepine, and Antoine Brousseau—applied jointly for adjoining land on the west bank of the Fraser River, a half-mile below the mouth of the Quesnel. Six years later the property was transferred to Mrs. Fabre Duclos and was subsequently subdivided as West Quesnel. Another Frenchman, Jean Brousseau, settled on a lake outside the town of Quesnel. He had been in the French Dragoons and that word became corrupted to "Dragon." His ranch was on Dragon Lake.

Still another interesting farmer was August Baker, born August Boulanger. When he and his brother Jean, or John as he was known, were naturalized they decided that they should have a Canadian name. Because *boulanger* is the French word for baker, that is what they chose to be called.

Property opposite the town of Quesnel and near the edge of Baker Creek, which runs into the Fraser from the mountains, was pre-empted by William Boucher on February 1, 1869. Part of his property, when granted, was reserved for a ferry site; the rest is now subdivided into town lots. Known locally as "Billy Bouchie," he had seen the hanging of the Indians in 1865. The name "Bouchie" has replaced the names "Henry's" or "Nigger" for the creek about four miles north of his pre-emption. The land where Bouchie

Creek empties into the river was taken by H. McDanus, M. McLain, and John K. Giscom in 1862. James Pollack, the liveryman, pre-empted to the east of these holdings. Moving north, Giscom operated a ferry on the Fraser at what became the lumber centre of Giscombe.

The town of Quesnel was located on the east side of the Fraser, between the two rivers. Frank "Doc" Trevor pre-empted 160 acres a quarter of a mile north of the townsite reserve, an area then known as "the Prairie." James Reid acquired Trevor's 1868 rights, and in 1914 Adam Barlow acquired the land. "Doc" Trevor was the first doctor resident in Quesnel, but farmed because he had so few patients.

The land which became known as North Quesnel—north of the townsite but south of Trevor's claim—was acquired by George W. Taylor in April 1869, and in 1900 by Mrs. Sarah Ann McLean, who had been the widow of Thomas Brown, partner of Hugh Gillis of the Occidental Hotel. Before this time, in October 1861, these two men, together with Donald McBride, had recorded claims for 160 acres each "contiguous to one another, situated on the north side of the Quesnel river and running up to the Fraser." This is lot 1557, the township of Quesnel. McBride wrote concerning this property when the townsite was reserved, but had had to accept the reservation. Brown and Gillis then made demands on the government, but when officials would not re-imburse them the two men took land two and a half miles to the north of the town. This land was later obtained by W. T. Ewing and still later by S. L. Hilborn.

Miners became fewer in number when the gold became less accessible and had to be extracted by huge machines. The exceedingly heavy loads of machinery going to the mines required larger freight wagons, and larger freight wagons required more horses to pull them. Farmers along the road therefore raised more horses and more feed for sale, and were able to maintain their economic balance, even though the number of people in the district needing food and housing declined.

Those ranchers who were situated directly beside the highway did quite well; they supplied food for both the miners and work animals. Later arivals, however, who had to settle away from the road or across the river—for instance, between Soda Creek and Quesnel on the west side of the Fraser—had a difficult time because they were farther from transportation.

In 1915 the Cariboo Farmers' Institute was formed to help

farmers solve the problems they would face when the railway reached the area and put an end to their feed business. By the time the railway ran through the country, the Institute had formulated plans for assisting farms and improving stock breeds. The Cariboo Agricultural and Horticultural Association had held the district's first fall fair and exhibition in September 1912. At that time they displayed those crops which could be grown locally, and later continued to work on improving produce. Over the years, the combined group efforts have brought about Illustration Stations at Quesnel's Fernbrook Farm and at Australian's Pleasant View Ranch, introduced selected breeding hogs, and advocated other projects, among them land clearing, slash burning, better Narcosli roads, and completion of the Pacific Great Eastern Railway.

The agricultural problems are the old ones of population and transportation. A great influx of new settlers did not come with the railway, and, despite government urging, the unemployed did not settle on farms during the depression. Farmers' worries had to be overcome by other means.

In 1938 the North Cariboo Growers' Co-operative Association established itself to market potatoes and other vegetables. A co-operative creamery had started in 1920 and Quesnel butter had been well known in the north, but this new association was expected to go further than the first. At first everything seemed to conspire to doom the infant society; several times, just as the concern had been rescued from debt, a fresh marketing or purchasing disaster arose. Most of the grief came from inexperience, a costly commodity. When Jack Rome became manager in 1944, however, the association began to achieve success. It now has a machinery line, owns its building and is agent for the Cariboo Certified Seed Potato Growers' Association, which was organized in 1946.

The seed potato industry came to the fore after World War II when many parts of British Columbia were plagued with potato blight while parts of Cariboo were disease free. The new interest was exceedingly well handled. By 1950, 420 acres of Cariboo land were producing one quarter of the total British Columbia seed potato crop, most of it coming from the Yorston property. One sixth of the seed potatoes produced were shipped to the United States. Unfortunately, in 1950 an early frost killed a great deal of the planting, in some areas as much as forty percent, and the following year lower prices prevailed. As a consequence, a combination of fear and frost together with an anticipated drop in prices curbed the increase in acreage.

Cattle in the area, apart from dairy herds, are not numerous, but Quesnel cattle sales do attract cattlemen from Anahim Lake and Nazko. Too, the town now has direct communication with the Chilcotin country where most of the beef is raised. The Quesnel Cattlemen's Association inaugurated a small sale with 275 head in 1947 figure, although in 1967 two sales were held with slightly fewer having been driven 200 miles from the Anahim area. The number of cattle sold varied slightly from year to year but not greatly from the 1947 figure, although in 1957 two sales were held with slightly fewer cattle being sold. In the entire Quesnel area, on both small holdings and on larger ranges fringing the Chilcotin, there are only about 6,000 cattle.

The cattle industry might thrive better on a feeder system; a farmer would fatten his few head on his own grain and sell them in the district. One obstacle to this system is a lack of cleared land on which to raise grain. The government gives a man clearing assistance in order to increase his present holdings, but machinery-rental costs absorb over $40 an acre. Although the landowners may repay the government on the instalment plan, they have cleared little land because both clearing land and maintaining that already cleared takes time.

For this reason farms are too small. In the past, to be economically self-supporting, farmers have had to subsidize their land with stopping houses or by mining, freighting, railway construction or logging. As a consequence, most farms are of a mixed variety, with 520 of them cultivating 20,800 acres of varied but not extensive field crops. Sheep do poorly because of predators, though the area west of the Fraser appears to be exceptionally promising for sheep. Chickens and turkeys are raised for local consumption, Christmas sales probably accounting for all the turkeys raised in Cariboo. And costs of imported feeds restrict both poultry and swine production.

Approximately 1,000 of the cattle in the district are dairy cows used by farm wives to supplement family incomes. For generations, farmers had raised milk cows for their own use, but when a creamery was built in 1920, only some of them shipped cream to it even though butter production never met demands. In 1945 G. E. Malcolm and F. D. Thomson opened Northern Dairy Products; the building contained a pasteurizing unit, milk cooler, compressors, bottle washers and cooling rooms to handle milk, cream, cottage cheese and buttermilk. The greatest problem facing the owners was that of persuading traditional cream producers to ship fluid milk and to keep the output at a year-round level (farmers are notorious for hating to milk cows throughout the winter). At the same time the Cariboo Farmers' Co-operative Association (Creamery) was purchasing cream from the farmers. This created a unique situation: the one group was shipping milk from Quesnel to be processed in Prince George and the other group was importing fluid milk from the Fraser Valley to Quesnel in order to meet local demands. The problem was resolved when Northern Dairy Products was sold.

The trouble is, once again, that of population. The Cariboo will remain agriculturally underdeveloped until British Columbia's more climatically favoured areas, with their easier working conditions, become overpopulated. Transportation costs, the high cost of imported feed, and a small consuming population retard the area's growth. The problem has not been disregarded. T. D. Patullo recognized it in 1937; Louis LeBourdais tried for years to promote an interest in Cariboo agriculture. But except for Veteran's Land Settlement, little new colonization has taken place.

One activity that might be considered either as agriculture or as manufacturing is flour milling, and with the growth of farms to feed a steadily increasing population of miners, Cariboo developed this subsidiary industry. High prices on imported commodities discouraged settlers and bulky goods were especially expensive because of freight rates. One of the most bulky in the food line was flour and the government often subsidized milling in order to reduce the price of flour.

The first flour mill established by private enterprise on the mainland colony was built at Dog Creek in 1861 by S. L. C. Brown and his partner, an expert millwright, Isadore Versepuche, frequently called Vespuies Gaspard. At first their flour was so poor that they almost went bankrupt but, faced with ruin, they made necessary milling changes and eventually sold a product of both good quality and colour. This was the Pioneer Mill which, when Brown moved it to Empire Valley, became known as "Excelsior Mill."

Barkerville was importing flour from Ashcroft or from the Bonaparte Valley and prices were high, but after Brown and Gaspard proved that good grain could be grown farther north, the general interest in milling increased. At Quesnellemouth, G. B. Wright was sufficiently interested to try to sell his sawmill in order to build a grist mill large enough to grind "50 bbls of flour in 24 hours." Because the government would not subsidize the project to the extent of £1,000 Wright did not build. Lillooet by that time had a second mill anyway and with the one at Dog Creek operating, the price of flour in Barkerville dropped from $1.50 a pound to just over 7¢. One of Wright's partners, Jerome Harper, went to Clinton and with J. H. Scott erected a mill there in 1868.

Even with this closer source of flour, mills were required nearer the mining populations. Knowing that if wheat planted at Williams Lake and Soda Creek were ground there freighters carrying it would have to pay fewer toll and transportation charges, the government offered assistance by allowing materials and machinery used in first construction to pass free of import duties and road tolls. Not only were the people of the interior interested, but so were those at the coast. The New Westminster Columbian carried news of W. H. Woodcock's selecting a site for a mill when in fact he had brought in new machines from California in 1866 and had stored them in New Westminster until the Soda Creek mill buildings were ready. That fall John R. Adams bought Woodcock's interest in the mill machinery and moved some of it north in December. The following April the Cariboo Sentinel recorded that "Mr. John R. Adams' Grist Mill is in running order and doing very good work." The flour was apparently of excellent quality and colour, but by early June the mill had ground all available grain and had to close until the 1867 crop was ready.

Of all the mills erected in the interior during the Colonial period, this one alone continued to operate. After converting from steam to water power in the first year of operation, the mill even shipped flour south to Yale and New Westminster by ox-team; empty wagons returning from the mines to Yale were available at low carrying charges. The mill was located on "Soda Creek at a point about 500 yards from its mouth...." It was on the Indian reserve, but a long term lease had been negotiated. In 1885 title to the mill site passed to J.F. Hawks. L. Krause operated it until 1942. The mill stood on the bank of the creek near the Cariboo Highway until it burned in 1947.

In 1868 R. A. Collins built and operated the Protection Mills using water from Deep (Hawk) Creek. He had pre-empted land on "both north and south banks of Deep Creek 4½ miles below Soda Creek," and located the mill there; by October 1868 his miller, John Marshall, was shipping to the mines. Ownership later passed to L. W. Patten who used the mill in the daytime for sawing lumber and at night for milling flour.

The next mill to operate was one on Fernbrook Farm across the Quesnel River from the townsite, at the confluence of the Fraser and Quesnel rivers. Operated by Senator James Reid and W. A. Johnston Sr. between 1887 and 1912, it was abandoned with the advent of cheap flour.

All mills in Cariboo were of the stone and roller type. The end of small flour and grist mills came when huge rollers were introduced on the prairies where wheat was cheap and plentiful. These roller mills manufactured a better quality flour of a better colour and at a price that forced small millers, like those of Cariboo, out of business.

Logging and lumbering are the industries attracting most attention in Cariboo today. Small farmers subsidize their farms by logging, and when logging is good, farming is poor. Lumbering is not new to the Quesnel area; it is almost as old as mining and agriculture, as old as the fur trade. Buildings first erected in the new areas were of log, with roofs added to replace the early sods, and then floors. The Hudson's Bay Company whipsawed lumber for the floors of buildings, and early miners whipsawed boards; closer to the mountains the men split good planks or shakes from easily obtained cedar.

Not long after the arrival of the miners who were busy men, with little time for anything but gold, an enterprising man named R. P. Baylor erected a sawmill at Antler where the first house in the region built entirely of boards appeared. Under the management of William Armstrong the mill worked by water from Antler Creek and supplied the required lumber for this most important centre. Judge Begbie wrote of economic conditions in Antler:

> Antler though in itself not well situated either in point of central locality with reference to the other Creeks, or as affording favourable line for Trails in any respect, distance, feed, or hard ground, may be considered as the headquarters of the Cariboo in 1861; there were from 60 to 70 houses in immediate contiguity, many of considerable size and cost and many more scattered up and down the valley; there was a larger population in this Valley probably than in any Town in the colony. There is a also a Saw Mill 1½ mile distant; the shops were well furnished: and there were articles of luxury which probably could not be obtained elsewhere beyond New Westminster, e.g. Champagne at $12 per bottle, etc.

Antler was the centre of Cariboo in 1861, but not in 1862. Richfield superseded Antler not only because the strikes were greater there, but also because rumours were already rampant that a road was to be constructed through Alexandria, Quesnellemouth, and on to the mines by way of the Cottonwood. The new centre at once had to have lumber. As Antler decayed, Richfield grew, and two sawmills supplied boards for the new roaring city of false fronts. One of the mills was Baylor's, moved from Antler.

Having influence, money and perhaps inside information about the route of the new road, G. B. Wright built a sawmill in partnership with Jerome Harper at the mouth of the Quesnel. Originally the mill was needed to cut lumber for a new and powerful steamer, the *Enterprise*. Operations began during the first week of December when the machinery arrived from Lillooet. Wright and Harper later became interested in flour mills. Quesnel was generally a one-sawmill town; as one closed another took its place. Some that were planned did not always materialize. As new steamships, stores and hotels appeared, a greater local demand for lumber arose. A certain amount of lumber was used for the huge boxes of the freight wagons; the box of a wagon which would make a return trip empty was often sold at the mines to be used for construction purposes. Because the mines themselves required timbers, the opportunistic "Billy" Ballou, his express service having failed, wrote to W. A. G. Young, the Colonial Secretary, for permission to import duty-free machinery for a water mill at Quesnel in order to cut lumber for flumes and ditches and other mining purposes. The Governor wrote that he could not grant this permission because he had "no power under existing law to exempt from duty dutiable goods."

The steam sawmill that had been erected at Quesnel was moved to Mink Gulch in 1866 by Meacham, Coombs and Nason. The following year a new one that could cut 1,000 feet a day began operating at Quesnel. The little hamlet was experiencing a period of boom with two water mills, each cutting 3,000 feet a day.

Every new event in the life of the area affected the economy. In January 1873 tenders were called to construct a bridge across the Quesnel River in order to replace the rope ferry. The contract went to D. F. Adams; he gave the lumber contract to W. A. Meacham and I. B. Nason who built a small mill at Quesnel. James Reid owned the first really permanent mill, which cut lumber for local use, but more especially for his Hixon Hills mining venture. Lumbering did not expand greatly until the construction of the Pacific Great Eastern Railway which required thousands of railway ties.

During the post-war boom of the 1920s considerable agitation for pulp mills arose and "proof" of great pulp mill opportunities appeared repeatedly. The lumbering boom in the area today came first from the world-wide demand for lumber, more than from the serious overcutting of coastal forests. During World War II coast mills were busy, too busy to supply a comparatively small interior market. Using portable and semi-portable mills which employed two, three or four men, inland British Columbia operators began developing their own lumber industry. Timber was small and more sparse than at the coast, but spruce and fir was acceptable to our Canadian prairie provinces and to the central United States. Big companies on the coast shunned these markets, and the interior operators were glad to get them. In 1942, Pacific Veneer Company of New Westminster became interested in the area and took birch for plywood. More important was this company's interest in the three- or four-hundred-year-old cottonwood trees, with their layers of bark that could be peeled easily without encountering knots—ideal for veneer. From the Agricultural and Horticultural Association, Pacific Veneer acquired two acres of land at the junction of the Quesnel and Fraser rivers for use as booming grounds for peeler logs, a collecting place for shipment to Vancouver. That same year thousands of cedar telephone poles were shipped from Horsefly and a new mill erected at Quesnel to cut birch for the coast furniture industry.

In the summer of 1945 a new industry gave the old town of Quesnel some of its 1865 appearance: "pit-propping." Sixty outfits invaded the area to cut pit-props for Welsh coal mines. Mostly located along the Nazko road, but with a centre at Hangman's Spring, they cut props in 5 to 8 foot lengths, a cord each day for $12.50. The cord brought $16 in Quesnel, where men loaded it into box cars and shipped it to tidewater.

Both the cottonwood peeler log industry and the pit-prop industry were hurt by the rising cost of labour. In addition, Britain's austerity program allowed no import of props from Canada when prices were rising here, but were reasonably stable in the Baltic countries. As a result, the Canadian pit-prop industry collapsed.

Pacific Veneer, taking six carloads of peeler logs from the Cottonwood area weekly, maintained its interest. In spite of considerable opposition from local sawmill operators who organized to prevent being squeezed by large holders, the company obtained a Forest Management licence in 1948. David Cromarty ran peeler logs down the Fraser River from north of Prince George for Western Plywoods (Cariboo) Limited at Quesnel and in 1950 this company was incorporated with a capital of $500,000 in order to operate a plywood plant in the town. The first log went through the mill on January 22, 1951 and the first plywood came off the hugh Siempelkamp bonding press on November 20th, the same year.

The rapid advance of the lumber industry in the first years of the decade is indicated by the number of registered sawmills within a thirty-mile radius of Quesnel. In 1948 there were 33 mills; by 1952 the number had grown to 180. Five planer mills were located in town. In 1958 while 6 planer mills were producing in town and 3 more within this radius, the total number of registered sawmills had dropped to 118; some of them were not operating, although others did operate on the outer fringes of the Quesnel forest district. In 1952, 71,000,000 board feet were produced and 127,000,000 feet in 1957. The increased payrolls added immeasurably to the local economy and brought new citizens to swell the population, even with the decline in both mills and production.

Sawmills, like mines, bring new people to an area. The short-lived pit-prop boom gave the town the air of a mining camp as each weekend the "pit-proppers" came to pitch tents on any available ground. Like agriculture, the lumber industry will develop only so long as population grows locally and world demand for lumber continues. Once the world demand slackens and once coastal mills are able to supply the demand, lumbering could become an activity of the past in Cariboo.

It is possible that the Cottonwood River may in time supply power to pulp mills—often rumoured as possible new industry. The river is estimated to have a potential of 402,000 horsepower, and the Quesnel River, 296,000 horsepower. From 1951 to 1953 a small supply of pulp-wood was cut for Powell River and sent by rail to a seaport, where it was loaded onto barges and carried to the mills there. In the case of pulp mills, as in the case of everything else, Quesnel never gives up hope. As late as 1956 Quesnel residents believed that a pulp mill would be constructed in Quesnel the next year, but the announcement was premature.

EPILOGUE

Though gold mining is now almost nonexistent, the legacy of gold remains forever. The creeks are quiet, but as a museum Barkerville lives on with more people walking the town streets than ever before, and the success of Barkerville as a museum must certainly say something about the dreams of gold. Gold brought people to Cariboo and, though many left without it, even some of those who left broke returned to try again and again. James Anderson wrote of heartbreak in 1868, but on almost any trip today a tourist can see a man with a pan by a creek. Mining, or reminders of mining, still lures the traveller to Cariboo: to thoughts of life in the less regulated world of Barkerville with its old church and its Theatre Royal, and Richfield with its Court House; to the red and yellow stage coaches and the claims marked with their unrealistic names—Neversweat, Mucho Oro and Alturis; to stories of Cariboo Cameron and his tragic marriage and of Georgina Wilhelmina Henrietta Nachtingall and her happy one to Joseph St. Laurent; to talk of sluices and of gulches, of creeks and bars and channels, and, of course, of mother lode.

The long-gone world lives on, an extension of the legend of the golden fleece and the argonauts who journey after it. Even today, when gold is mentioned in the Cariboo all work seems to stop. But as romantic as the gold rush might seem, it had a reality in the millions of dollars taken from those creeks and gulches, and that gold not only bolstered an economy, created a society, and attracted world wide attention, but also made British Columbia attractive to jubilant eastern Canadians who read in their newspapers that Victoria was "destined... to become one of the largest commercial harbours in the universe," that the Dominion had made "the acquisition of one of the wealthiest countries in the world," and that British Columbia would "increase in prosperity and wealth in such a manner as will astonish even the most sanguine expectant." Perhaps it was the gold rush which established British Columbians as brash and emotional small capitalists filled with energy, creativity, individuality. Someone has called British Columbia a land of restless growth and movement; someone else called it "improbable." Still others see British Columbia as a materialistic and classless frontier with an easy democracy in which one might still "strike it rich" either socially or economically. Fortunately that frontier also means freedom of thought, and freedom to dream.

And as the multiple riches of the huge domain of Cariboo are being rediscovered, and although the recent growth of the area has been with products and activities other than gold, the magic of gold lured men into the area, and oddly enough the magic of the word lights up their eyes today.

BIBLIOGRAPHY

Special Studies in *British Columbia Historical Quarterly:*

Hacking, Norman, "British Columbia Steamboat Days, 1870-1883," *BCHQ* 11:69-111, April, 1947.

———"Steamboats on the Fraser in the 'Sixties,'" *BCHQ* 10:1-41, January 1946.

Ireland, Willard E., "Early Flour-mills in British Columbia, Part 1," *BCHQ* 5:191-213, July 1941.

———"Hudson's Bay Company Lands on the Mainland of British Columbia. 1858-1861," *BCHQ* 3:75-99, April 1939.

———"Some Pioneers of the Cattle Industry," *BCHQ* 6:257-275, October 1942.

LeBourdais, Louis, "Billy Barker of Barkerville," *BCHQ* 1:165-170, July 1937.

MacKay, Corday, "The Collins Overland Telegraph," *BCHQ* 10:187-215, July 1946.

Pettit, Sydney G., "'Dear Sir Matthew': A Glimpse of Judge Begbie," *BCHQ* 11:1-14, January 1947.

———"His Honour's Honour: Judge Begbie and the Cottonwood Scandal," *BCHQ* 11:187-210, July 1947.

———"Judge Begbie in Action: The Establishment of Law and Preservation of Order in British Columbia," *BCHQ* 11:187-210, July 1947.

———"The Tyrant Judge: Judge Begbie in Court," *BCHQ* 11:273-294, October 1947.

Reid, Robie L., "Captain Evans of Cariboo," *BCHQ* 2:233-246, October 1938.

West, Willis, J., "The 'B.X.' and the Rush to Fort George," *BCHQ* 13:129-229, July-October 1949.

———"Staging and Stage Hold-ups in the Cariboo," *BCHQ* 12:185-209, July 1948.

Books:

Doughty, A. G., and Lanctot, G., eds., *Cheadle's Journal of a Trip Across Canada*, 1862-63, Ottawa, Graphic, 1931.

Harmon, Daniel Williams, *A Journal of Voyages and Travels in the Interior of North America*, New York, Barnes, 1903.

Jennings, Tess E., trans., "Report on the Missions of the Diocese of Quebec." July 1845. Number 6. (Typescript)

Johnson, R. Byron, *Very Far West Indeed*, London, Sampson Low..., 1872.

McInnes, Alexander P., *Chronicles of the Cariboo*...., Lillooet, Lillooet Publishers, [1938].

Morice, A. G., *The History of the Northern Interior of British Columbia*, Toronto, William Briggs, 1904.

Masson, L. R., *Le Bourgeois de la Compagnie Nord-ouest*, A. Coté et Cie, 1889.

Palmer, H. Spencer, *Report of a Journey of Survey from Victoria to Fort Alexandria, via North Bentinck Arm*, New Westminster, Royal Engineers Press, 1863.

———*Williams Lake and Cariboo Report* (on portions of the) *Williams Lake and Cariboo Districts and on the Fraser River from Fort Alexandria to Fort George*, New Westminster, Royal Engineers Press, 1863.

Ross, Victor, *A History of the Canadian Bank of Commerce*, Toronto, Oxford University Press, 1920, vol. 1.

Runnalls, F. E., *A History of Prince George*, Vancouver, Wrigley, 1946.

Wade, M. S., *The Overlanders of '62*, Victoria, King's Printer, 1931.

Walkem, W. Wymond, M.D., *Stories of Early British Columbia*, Vancouver, News Advertiser, 1914.

Wallace, W. S., ed., *John McLean's Notes of a Twenty Five Year's Service in the Hudson's Bay Territory*, Toronto, Champlain Society, 1932.

INDEX

Printed in the United States
By Bookmasters